Victims of the Miracle

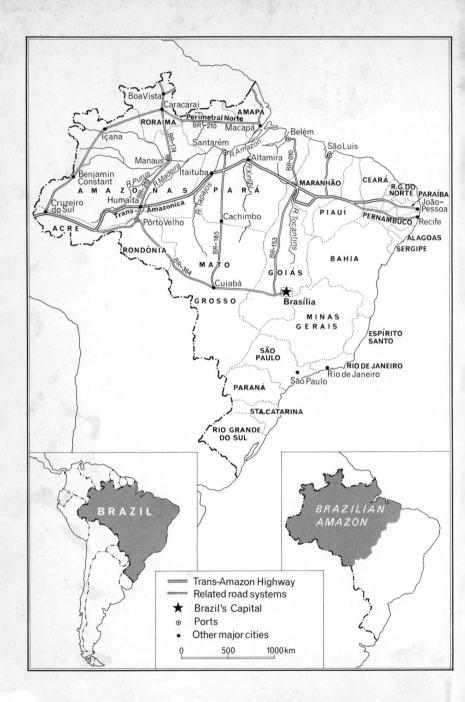

Trans-Amazon Highway
Related road systems
★ Brazil's Capital
⊙ Ports
● Other major cities

0   500   1000km

Victims of the Miracle

Development and the Indians of Brazil

SHELTON H. DAVIS

Director, Anthropology Resource Center
Cambridge, Massachusetts

CAMBRIDGE UNIVERSITY PRESS

Cambridge
London   New York   Melbourne

Published by the Syndics of the Cambridge University Press
The Pitt Building, Trumpington Street, Cambridge CB2 1RP
Bentley House, 200 Euston Road, London NW1 2DB
32 East 57th Street, New York, NY 10022, USA
296 Beaconsfield Parade, Middle Park, Melbourne 3206, Australia

First published 1977
Reprinted 1978
Printed in the United States of America
Typeset, printed, and bound by Vail-Ballou Press, Inc.,
Binghamton, New York

Library of Congress Cataloging in Publication Data

Davis, Shelton H

Victims of the miracle.

Bibliography: p.

Includes index.

1. Indians of South America – Brazil – Government relations.
2. Brazil – Economic conditions – 1945–
3. Human ecology – Amazon Valley.   I. Title.
F2519.3.G6D38   301.45'19'8081   77–5132

ISBN 0 521 21738 5   hard covers
ISBN 0 521 29246 8   paperback

To the memory of my father, Robert Davis,
and to my mother, Fannie Secher Davis,
for their compassion, generosity, and concern.

Contents

Tables

Maps

Preface
and acknowledgments

Over the past few years, several books have been written on the controversial question of Indian policy in Brazil. In 1973, Robin Hanbury-Tenison, founder of Survival International of London, published a book titled, *A Question of Survival for the Indians of Brazil*. This was followed by a report for the Aborigines Protection Society of London by Edwin Brooks, René Fuerst, John Hemming, and Francis Huxley, titled, *Tribes of the Amazon Basin in Brazil, 1972*. More recently, two American scientists, Robert J. A. Goodland and Howard S. Irwin, have published a small monograph, *Amazon Jungle: Green Hell to Red Desert?*, which includes a chapter on the situation of Indian tribes in the Amazon Basin of Brazil. The present book differs from all the above accounts in emphasizing the political and economic factors that are bringing about the uprooting and demise of Brazilian Indian tribes.

The central contention of this book is that the massive amount of disease, death, and human suffering unleashed upon Brazilian Indians in the past few years is a direct result of the economic development policies of the military government of Brazil. In broadest terms, what I wish to demonstrate is how the present situation of Brazilian Indians is structurally related to the much acclaimed, but little understood, "economic miracle" in Brazil. In order to do so, I focus major attention on the economic development policies of the Brazilian military regime.

xi

In the pages of this book, I provide detailed documentation of various instances where large private, state, and multinational corporations, the principal ingredients in the Brazilian model of development, have systematically expropriated Indian resources. I also argue that Brazilian Indians are only the first victims (albeit the most powerless) of a particular economic progress that also includes the victimization of hundreds of agricultural and highway workers in the Amazon, thousands of dispossessed rural migrants from the Brazilian Northeast, and millions of poor and hungry people who live in the large Brazilian cities of São Paulo and Rio de Janeiro. Finally, through an analysis of the ecological chain reaction set in motion by the deforestation of the Brazilian Amazon, I show what the implications of this program are for the biosphere and the earth.

Most generally, this book attempts to analyze what happens when modern forms of capitalist development begin to penetrate one of the last and largest frontier regions of the Americas. Like the notion of "Civilization" that was so popular in the latter half of the nineteenth century, "Development" is one of those terms that is taken for granted as a necessary good by most governments, planners, and publics today. The mystique surrounding the notion of "Economic Development" is so great that most people tend to assume that it will benefit all peoples, regions, and nations throughout the world.

Nowhere is this uncritical acceptance more prevalent than in the case of present-day Brazil. The impressive growth rate of the Brazilian economy, surpassing that of the United States in the latter part of the nineteenth century and that of Japan in the postwar period, is accepted by most foreign observers as indicative of a positive good for the people of Brazil. As a result, few observers have analyzed the institutional structure of the Brazilian political economy: the alliances that have emerged in Brazil between domestic capitalists and multinational firms, the dominant role of a repressive military government in generating capital formation and economic growth, and the significance of technological transfers and international aid in bringing about the Brazilian "economic miracle." Similarly, little consideration has been given by outside observers to the social implications and costs of this economic growth. Few observers, for example, have questioned who has benefited from the Brazilian "economic miracle" and which social sectors have necessarily suffered and lost.

In this book, I analyze the human and ecological consequences of neocapitalist development in the Amazon region of Brazil. Rather than assume that the economic development of the Brazilian Amazon is a positive good, I attempt to assess what this particular model of development has meant for the peoples of the region, and what will be the long-term effects of this development on the delicate ecology of the Amazon rain forest.

Most contemporary accounts of conditions in the Brazilian Amazon have failed to trace the specific linkages that exist between the development policies of the Brazilian government and the threats posed to Indian peoples and the environment. These linkages, I believe, are critical. Hence, in this book, I have focused upon what processes of neocapitalist development in the Amazon have meant for the welfare of Indian communities, the large rural and urban populations of Brazil, and the tropical ecosystem. To the reader who is familiar with recent activities in other frontier areas of the world, generated in large measure by the supposed energy, food, and resource crises, it will be obvious that the processes that I describe go far beyond the single case of Brazil.

By way of preface, I wish to acknowledge the many friends who assisted me in the conception of this book. My original concern with the situation of Brazilian Indians dates back to 1969, when I was a visiting instructor in anthropology at the National Museum in Rio de Janeiro. At that time, I had just completed two years of ethnographic fieldwork in Guatemala and was interested in the study of agrarian systems in Latin America. During the final months of my work at the National Museum, I met a Brazilian physician named Noel Nutels. Noel Nutels had spent more than twenty-five years providing medical assistance to Brazilian Indian tribes, and during the last months of the government of Brazilian President João Goulart served as director of the Indian Protection Service in Brazil.

In October 1970, Noel Nutels came to the National Museum seeking support from Brazilian and foreign anthropologists in order to protest the new Brazilian Indian Statute that was announced at the time of the inauguration of the Trans-Amazon Highway. The general political climate in Brazil at this time made it difficult for my Brazilian colleagues to take any organized action against Indian policy along the new Amazon roads. My own position as a foreign anthropologist, however, was different, and I said that I would assist him in making these issues known. He was particularly concerned that continuing attention be focused upon Brazilian Indian policy by anthropologists in Europe and the United States.

During my final weeks in Brazil, I talked to Noel Nutels on several occasions and through his personal knowledge gained an immense amount of insight into the history of Indian policy in Brazil. In February 1973, Noel Nutels died of cancer, a few days after Orlando and Claudio Villas Boas, two of his closest friends and Brazil's best-known Indian agents, made contact with the Kréen-Akaróre tribe. In seeking the causes for the misnamed "Indian Problem" in Brazil in political and economic factors, I have drawn heavily upon the ideas and work of Noel Nutels. My debt to the Brazilian anthropologist Darcy Ribeiro, another close friend and colleague of Noel Nutels, is discussed in Chapter 1 of this book.[1]

In January 1971, I returned to the United States, and began to carry out systematic research on Indian policy in Brazil. During this time, I also began to collaborate with two anthropologists who had done field research in Brazil. One of these anthropologists was Kenneth Brecher of the Institute of Social Anthropology at Oxford University, who at the time was living with the Waurá tribe in the Xingu National Park. The other was Patrick Menget, an instructor at the University of Nanterre in France, who had lived with the Txikão tribe, also in the Xingu Park.

The appreciation I possess of the Indian societies of Brazil comes through long discussions with Kenneth Brecher and Patrick Menget. The rich tribal ways of life that they described to me often led me to reflect upon my own experiences in the Mayan-speaking community of Santa Eulalia in Guatemala where I lived for two years. My debt to these two anthropologists is lasting and great. They are not, however, to be held accountable in any way for the statements made in this book.

In September 1971, I began to teach at Harvard University, where I gave a course on the Indian tribes of the United States. During this period, I made contact with a number of Native American students, and began to see the parallels between the historic situation of Indians across the American continent. At the same time I also made contact with Marie-Helene Laraque, who was mobilizing support for the cause of Brazilian Indians among native leaders in Canada and the United States.

In 1973, I moved to Berkeley, California, and was there a cofounder with Marie-Helene Laraque of a documentation and information center on these issues called INDIGENA. IN-DIGENA is the Spanish and Portuguese word for Native American and was established for two purposes. First, to generate international concern for the critical situation of Indians in the Amazon Basin of South America; and second, to create a reciprocal exchange of information between native peoples and organizations across the American continent. Marie-Helene Laraque and her husband Walter Carlin, who was born on the Cheyenne River (Sioux) Reservation in South Dakota, contributed in numerous ways to the development of the position expressed in this book.

While working with INDIGENA in Berkeley, I also collaborated with two other organizations, the North American

Congress on Latin America (NACLA) and the *Brazilian Information Bulletin* (BIB). All these organizations shared a concern with the role of U.S. foreign policy and multinational corporation activities in Latin America. Most of the documentation from business journals contained in this book, as well as my general research methodology, came through the collaboration of the staffs of INDIGENA, NACLA, and BIB.[2]

Through the assistance of these organizations, I began to collect a file of documents on the contemporary political economy of Brazil, the scope of foreign aid and investment in the Amazon, and the nature of development and Indian policies in Brazil. This material was drawn from trade journals, government reports, and newspapers; hence, they differ in quality and reliability from the primary materials gathered through ethnographic fieldwork by anthropologists. I have tried to alleviate these problems of reliability by working like a historian or investigative journalist interested in a contemporary social issue. This involved double checking my sources of information and corresponding with persons who have been to the Amazon and could verify certain facts. I have intentionally provided a detailed documentation in the notes at the end of the book for the reader interested in checking the accuracy of my sources, data, and facts.

The discussions of recent mining projects in the Amazon contained in Chapters 3, 6, and 7 of this book could not have been written without the original research on this subject done by Fred Goff and Marsha Miliman, which first appeared in *NACLA's Latin America and Empire Report* (April 1973). Likewise, almost everything contained in Chapter 8 on agribusiness activities in the Brazilian Amazon came from long discussions with my close friend, Paul Silberstein. The latter shared with me his experience growing up on a farm in the birthplace of modern agribusiness (Southern California) and his several years of research on the structure of commercial agriculture in Brazil.

Three anthropologists who teach in the University of California system also encouraged me in this work. The first was Joseph

G. Jorgensen, director of the Program in Comparative Culture at the University of California at Irvine. Joseph Jorgensen was the first American anthropologist to analyze conditions of poverty and underdevelopment on American Indian Reservations in terms of the expanding political economy of the United States. He was also the first anthropologist to use Andre Gunder Frank's "metropolis-satellite" hypothesis, developed in Latin America to explain class and ethnic inequalities in the American West. For several years, my own work has benefited from Joseph Jorgensen's commentary, criticism, and advice. In many respects, this book can be seen as an international extension of the conceptual framework contained in his North American research.[3]

The other two anthropologists who provided encouragement for my work were Laura Nader and Gerald D. Berreman of the University of California at Berkeley. The emphasis I place on government and corporate activities in the Brazilian Amazon reflects Laura Nader's notion that anthropologists should be studying "up" rather than "down," and investigating the powerful political, economic, and legal institutions that have created so much "endemic powerlessness" in the modern world.[4] The idea of relating events in the Brazilian Amazon to wider social issues arose from several discussions with Gerald Berreman on the value of critical anthropological research.[5] Gerald Berreman was particularly helpful in a careful reading of an earlier draft of this book.

Over the past several years, I have also benefited from long discussions with Paul Shankman of the University of Colorado at Boulder. In editing the final draft of this book, I have been assisted by Timothy Buckalew, James Ito-Adler, and Robert Mathews. Robert Mathews provided me with invaluable assistance in questions of argument, presentation, and style.

Finally, I wish to thank Ralph Nader and Ruth Fort of the Center for the Study of Responsive Law in Washington, D.C. As far back as 1970, Ralph Nader spoke out on the need for international action to counter the atrocities being committed against

Indians in South America. Then, in February 1974, he asked INDIGENA to prepare a report for him on the scope of American aid and investment programs in the Brazilian Amazon. This was followed in November 1974 with a press conference in Washington on the subject of "Brazilian Indian Policy: The Need for International Action and Concern."[6]

Perhaps more than any other experience, working with Ralph Nader and Ruth Fort taught me that information in and of itself is of minor importance. In any society that claims to be based on the democratic participation of its citizenry, such information must be translated into strategies of public action, accountability, and change. The information and documentation contained in this book is written from exactly this point of view.

The spelling of tribal names in this book follows the convention instituted by the First Reunion of Brazilian Anthropology, published in the *Revista de Antropologia*, vol. 2 (São Paulo, 1954), pp. 150–2. In a small number of cases, I have changed the spelling of tribal names in accord with suggestions made by Robert Carneiro of the American Museum of Natural History. For conventional English spellings of Brazilian tribal names, the reader should also consult the maps and tables in Janice H. Hopper (ed.), *Indians of Brazil in the Twentieth Century* (Washington, D.C., 1967).

S. H. D.

Cambridge, Massachusetts
April 1977

1

Brazilian Indian policy: an historical overview

The country along this river is a fine natural cattle country, and someday it will surely see a great development. It was opened to development by Colonel Rondon only five or six years ago. Already an occasional cattle ranch is to be found along the banks. When the railroads are built into these interior portions of Mato Grosso, the whole region will grow and thrive amazingly – and so will the railroads.

Theodore Roosevelt, Through the Brazilian Wilderness (1914)

At the beginning of this century, a wave of interethnic violence and conflict encompassed the southern regions of Brazil. During this period, Indians and pioneers contested vast areas of territory along Brazil's newly opened frontiers. In the forested area south of the Doce River and in the states of Minas Gerais and Espírito Santo, Botocudo Indians resisted the invasion of their tribal territory and were nearly successful in forcing the abandonment of an Italian-settler colony at São Mateus. In the State of São Paulo, Kaingáng Indians interrupted the construction of the Brazil Northwest Railroad and maintained control over a 200-mile area between the Tietê, Feio, Peixe, and Paranapanema rivers. Farther to the south, in the Brazilian states of Paraná and Santa Catarina, colonization companies paid professional Indian killers to massacre the Xokléng tribe.[1]

News of these conflicts filled the pages of the national press and caused a bitter and highly political debate in Brazil. During this period, several professors of German descent were teaching

1

racist social theories in the universities of São Paulo, and a number of continental missions called for immediate government action to protect the lives of European settlers in Brazil. The influence of these foreign elements was so great that the president of Brazil held several cabinet meetings to study the possibility of using the Brazilian Army to stop conflicts along the frontier. In the Brazilian Congress, a number of legislators argued that it was expedient, for purposes of national development, to use the same extermination tactics against Indians as those practiced by the U.S. military in the occupation of much of North America.[2]

At the same time, however, another group emerged that was horrified by reports of the massacre of Indian tribes. Many of these people were of upper-class background and belonged to scientific and philanthropic societies. Strongly influenced by French positivism, they vehemently reacted against the various pseudoscientific and racist theories that were gaining influence among cosmopolitan circles in Brazil. It was the responsibility of the government, they argued, to provide protection for the remaining Indian populations of the country. In time, these people believed, Indians would also take their place as citizens in the newly independent and republican nation of Brazil.[3]

The major spokesman for this position was a young Brazilian Army officer named Cândido Mariano da Silva Rondon. Rondon was born in 1865 in the small interior town of Cuiabá, Mato Grosso, and as a youth attended military school in Rio de Janeiro. There he studied engineering and came under the influence of the positivist writings of the French social philosopher Auguste Comte. Today, Comte's philosophy of social evolution seems archaic and ethnocentric. At the end of the last century, however, it provided Rondon with a convincing philosophic framework for understanding the Indian societies that he had known through experience and observation as a youth.[4]

In 1890, the Brazilian government commissioned Rondon to carry out a series of military and scientific expeditions to the unexplored interior regions of the country. These expeditions lasted over a twenty-five-year period and received a large amount of publicity both in Brazil and abroad. During the course of these expeditions, the Rondon Commission laid over 2,270 kilometers of telegraph lines, mapped over 50,000 square kilometers of land, and discovered twelve new rivers in the Mato Grosso and Amazon regions of Brazil. In 1913, Rondon accompanied former American President Theodore Roosevelt on his world-famous geographical expedition through the wilderness regions of Brazil.[5]

In the course of these expeditions, Rondon also made contact with the Borôro, Nambikuára, and Paresí Indian tribes. For Rondon, these Indian societies were neither savage nor barbarian, but merely one stage in the overall development of human civilization. Rondon argued that the authenticity and value of these tribal societies could not be doubted and that it was the responsibility of the government to provide aboriginal peoples with the conditions needed for survival. A number of other young army officers shared his humanistic philosophy. In 1910, these officers were successful in convincing the government to create a special agency for the protection of Indian tribes.

The government named Colonel Rondon the first director of the new Indian Protection Service (SPI). As its name implied, the SPI was not an agency charged with the administration of Indian affairs, but rather was an institution whose purpose was to protect Indians against acts of frontier persecution and oppression. The legislation that established the SPI, and which was later included in several Brazilian constitutions, explicitly stated that it was the obligation of the Brazilian government to protect Indians against the destructive effects of frontier expansion and to defend their lives, liberty, and property against extermination and exploitation. In addition, this legislation recognized the rights of Indian peoples to exist on their own lands and to continue, under the guardianship of the government, their ancient and traditional ways of life.[6]

The most novel aspect of this new policy was the intervention of the Indian Protection Service in the occupation and settlement of vast areas of Brazil. Under the direction of Rondon, a unique strategy developed for making contact with and pacifying formerly hostile Indian tribes. The basic notion behind this strategy was to convince Indians that the government was different from all other agents along the frontier. Teams of unarmed Indian agents, almost all of whom shared the philosophy and dedication of Rondon, would enter into Indian territories and place gifts of beads, machetes, and mirrors at the entrances to Indian villages. There they would wait patiently, sometimes for weeks or months, until the Indians would come forward and accept the gifts. Then, after a period of time, the agents would enter the villages and, using Indian interpreters, try to convince the native chiefs that the intention of the government was to protect them from outside encroachments and pioneer threats.

During this early period, the motto of the Indian Protection Service was "Die if it be necessary, but kill never." Using this pacifistic approach, scores of Indian tribes were brought under the direction and protection of the SPI. In the first two decades of its existence, the SPI created sixty-seven Indian posts in various frontier zones of Brazil.

According to the Brazilian anthropologist Darcy Ribeiro, the SPI lived up to the pacifistic ideals of Rondon during this early period. In the first twenty years of its existence, not a single Indian was killed or wounded by Indian agents, although several Indian agents died. Among the tribes pacified during this early period were the Kaingáng of São Paulo and Paraná (1912), whose lands are now covered by productive coffee plantations; the Botocudos (1914) of the Itajaí Valley, which is now one of the richest regions of Santa Catarina State; the Aimoré (1911) of the Rio Doce Valley in Minas Gerais and Espírito Santo, an area now occupied by towns, industries, and farms; the Umutina (1918) of the Sepotuba and Paraguay rivers, whose pacification made possible the exploitation of the large ipecac forests of Brazil; the Parintintín (1922), who had prevented the exploitation of large rubber tracts along the Madeira River and its tributaries; and the Urubús (1928), who had caused turmoil throughout the entire Gurupí Valley between Pará and Maranhão.

Nevertheless, as Ribeiro also notes, "the job of pacifying Indians was designed less for them than for Brazilian society as a whole." In case after case, Indians accepted the gifts and promises of government agents only to find that their territories were later invaded by rubber collectors, nut gatherers, cattle ranchers, and settlers along the Brazilian frontiers. The SPI tried to mediate in these encounters by establishing Indian posts in several areas, but more often than not Indian agents were ineffective in holding back settlers and in influencing state governments to provide legal titles for Indian lands. As a result, in almost every area of Brazil where the SPI functioned, Indians were wiped out by disease or became marginalized ethnic populations on minuscule parcels of land.[7]

The situation of Brazilian Indians (1957)

In 1957, Ribeiro published a lengthy statistical report on the situation of Indian tribes in Brazil. The study showed that from 1900 to 1957 more than eighty Indian tribes came in contact with Brazilian national society and through disease and contamination were deculturated and destroyed. During this period, the indigenous population of Brazil dropped from approximately 1 million to less than 200,000. In areas of agricultural expansion, six aboriginal tribes became extinct. In areas of pastoral expansion (cattle raising), thirteen tribes disappeared. In areas of extractive activities (rubber and nut collecting, diamond prospecting, etc.), a phenomenal fifty-nine Indian tribes were destroyed.[8]

The threatened extinction of the last remaining Indian peoples of Brazil was only a small part of the picture given in this report.

Ribeiro showed that those tribes that had survived the initial depredations of the expanding Brazilian frontier were severely depopulated and living in the most wretched conditions.

The Kaingáng of São Paulo, for example, were reduced from 1,200 persons at the time of their pacification in 1912 to a mere 87 ragged and starving individuals in 1957. The Xokléng of Santa Catarina were reduced from over 800 to less than 190. The Nambikuára of Mato Grosso were reduced from an estimated 10,000 to less than 1,000. The once proud and thriving Kayapó Indians living in the region of Conceição de Araguaia in northern Mato Grosso were reduced from 2,500 at the time of contact in 1902 to less than 10 in 1957. Along the borders between the states of Pará and Maranhão in the Gurupí Valley, the Tembé and Timbíra tribes, whose population was estimated to number between 6,000 and 7,000 in a census of 1872, were reduced by 1957 to three villages of less than 20 persons each.

Ribeiro classified the remaining Indian tribes of Brazil into four categories depending upon their degree of contact with the agents of Brazilian society: relative isolation, intermittent contact, permanent contact, and integration. Tribes that had moved from a state of relative isolation to *intermittent contact* with Brazilian society numbered twenty-seven in Ribeiro's sample and were suffering the worst effects of disease and depopulation. In his report, Ribeiro wrote:

Judging by known cases, the decimating effects of epidemics of grippe, measles, and other morbid agents carried by civilized peoples would have reduced their population by at least half of what it was while they were still isolated. There had been thoroughgoing transformations in their way of life, changes attributable to ecological and biotic factors rather than to the process of acculturation.[9]

According to Ribeiro, many of these tribes in intermittent contact with Brazilian society had developed strategies to deal with the new and dangerous invaders in their midst. Some tribes escaped into the jungles or unwanted refuge areas as a last retreat. Other tribes attempted to stand their ground and resist. Basically, all these tribes were attempting to maintain their independence in the face of an ever-increasing outside threat.

A similar situation faced the forty-five tribes Ribeiro classified as being in *permanent contact* with Brazilian national society. Population decline in these groups was also severe. The social organization and ceremonial lives of these tribes had been disrupted. Old patterns of cooperation had been broken down. Native subsistence systems had been undermined. These peoples had become dependent upon Brazilian national society and were forced to participate in the various regional economies of Brazil. Ribeiro noted that:

Unlike the tribal Indian, the individual living in permanent contact was dependent upon the national society as an individual rather than a group member. Freed from the ancient system of social control by the breakdown of tribal sanctions, the group was headed for disintegration.[10]

The step from permanent contact to *integration* into Brazilian national society produced no better conditions for the surviving Indians of Brazil. Ribeiro wrote of these integrated tribes:

At the turn of the century, their economic role was that of a reserve labor force, or of specialized producers of certain marketable commodities. They were an unwanted minority, restricted to segments of the lands they had formerly held or cast out of territory rightfully theirs and forced to roam from place to place.[11]

These integrated tribes numbered thirty-eight in 1957, and, in Ribeiro's words, "were enduring the most precarious conditions of life in the greatest misery." They had forgotten their ancient languages and customs, and were living as wretched and marginalized ethnic groups at the bottom layer of Brazilian rural society. Faced by discrimination and exploitation, these integrated tribes found it impossible to assimilate into Brazilian national life. "Some imponderable obstacle," Ribeiro wrote, "blocked their assimilation. There was a final step that they were unable to take."[12]

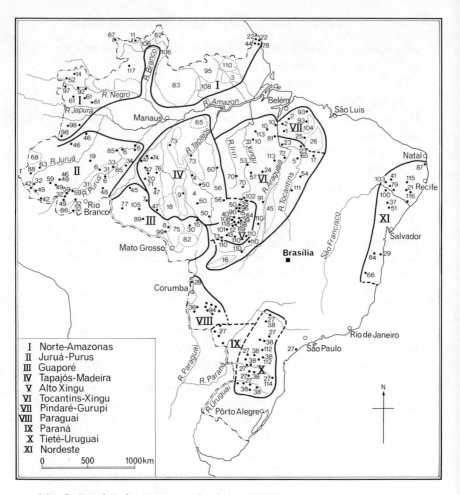

Map 2. Brazil: Indian groups and culture areas

Key to indigenous groups of Brazil:

1 Amaneyé	11 Awake	21 Fulnió	31 Jamamadí
2 Anambe	12 Awéti	22 Galibí	32 Jamináwa
3 Aparaí	13 Bakairí	23 Gavião	33 Jaruára
4 Apiaká	14 Baníwa	24 Gorotíre	34 Júma
5 Apinayé	15 Beiço-de-Pau	25 Guajá	35 Jurúna
6 Apurinã	16 Borôro	26 Guajajára	36 Kadiwéu
7 Arara	17 Canela	27 Guaraní	37 Kaimbé
8 Arikapú	18 Cinta-Larga	28 Guató	38 Kaingáng
9 Aripaktsá	19 Deni	29 Gueren	39 Kalapálo
10 Asuriní	20 Diarrói	30 Irantxe	40 Kamayurá

The culture areas legend on the map:

I Norte-Amazonas
II Juruá-Purus
III Guaporé
IV Tapajós-Madeira
V Alto Xingu
VI Tocantins-Xingu
VII Pindaré-Gurupi
VIII Paraguai
IX Paraná
X Tieté-Uruguai
XI Nordeste

0   500   1000 km

In 1957, the major concentration of indigenous population was still in the Amazon and central regions of Brazil. Over 120 Indian tribes inhabited this immense area, living in small tribal groups that numbered between 100 and 500 individuals (see Map 2). Most of these tribes still subsisted from hunting, fishing, and gardening activities and maintained close attachments to their ancestral territories. The fate of these *isolated* tribes, Ribeiro argued, would depend upon two factors: (1) the nature of future economic expansion in Brazil; and (2) the ability of the Indian Protection Service to create a protective buffer between Indians and the frontiers of national society. Without such protection, Ribeiro claimed, the remaining isolated Indian tribes of Brazil would be contaminated by disease and eventually disappear.[13]

At the time of Ribeiro's study, several important changes were taking place in Indian policy in Brazil. From the postwar period onward, Indian policy was increasingly tied to regional and na-

---

Map 2. Key (*cont.*)

41 Kambiwá	61 Makú	81 Parakanân	100 Tuxá
42 Kámpa	62 Makuxí	82 Paresí	101 Txikão
43 Karajá	63 Marúbo	83 Parukotó-	102 Txukahamae
44 Karipúna	64 Matipuhy	Xarúma	103 Uamué
45 Karitiâna	65 Mawé	84 Pataxó	104 Urubú
46 Katukína	66 Maxakalí	85 Paumarí	105 Urupá
47 Kawahib	67 Mayongóng	86 Piro	106 Wapitxana
48 Kaxararí	68 Mayoruna	87 Potiguára	107 Waríkyana
49 Kaxináwa	69 Mehináku	88 Poyanáwa	108 Waurá
50 Kayabí	70 Menkranotire	89 Puruborá	109 Wayâna
51 Kirirí	71 Morerébi	90 Suyá	110 Xavante
52 Kobéwa	72 Mudjetíre	91 Tapirapé	111 Xerénte
53 Kokraimoro	73 Mundurukú	92 Tariána	112 Xetá
54 Krahó	74 Mura	93 Tembé	113 Xikrín
55 Krikatí	75 Nambikuára	94 Terêna	114 Xokléng
56 Kréen-Akaróre	76 Numbiaí	95 Tiriyo-Pianokoto	115 Xukurú
57 Kubén-Kran-	77 Pakahanova	96 Trumái	116 Xukurú-
Kegn	78 Palikúr	97 Tukána	Kariří
58 Kuikúru	79 Pankarare	98 Tukúna	117 Yanomamö
59 Kulína	80 Pankararú	99 Tuparí	118 Yawalapiti
60 Kuruáya			

Source: "Indigenous Groups of Brazil," in W. Dostal (ed.), *The Situation of the Indian in South America* (Geneva, 1972), pp. 434–42.

tional politics. By this time, Rondon was an old man, and he and many of his dedicated collaborators had lost influence over Indian affairs. Then, in the late 1950s, a new group of army officers and civil servants began to assume positions of power in the SPI.

During this period, a wave of bureaucratic corruption infested the administration of the SPI. The new SPI regime disbanded the Section of Anthropological Studies that Darcy Ribeiro had helped to create in the early 1950s. It entrusted several Indian posts to religious missionaries. It tolerated pacification expeditions that were detrimental to the welfare and safety of Indian tribes. It maintained very little control over the activities of Indian agents along the national frontiers. In simplest terms, during this period, economic rather than humanitarian considerations began to form the basis of Indian policy in Brazil.[14]

The Figueiredo Report (1968)

In 1967, the significance of these new directives became clear when world attention focused on Indian policy in Brazil. Previous to this date only a few people outside Brazil were concerned with Brazilian Indian policy. Then, in 1967, the Brazilian minister of the interior, General Albuquerque Lima, commissioned Attorney General Jader Figueiredo to carry out an investigation of charges of corruption among officials of the Indian Protection Service. Figueiredo and his staff of investigators traveled over 10,000 miles, interviewing scores of Indian agents, and visiting over 130 Indian posts. Finally, in March 1968, General Albuquerque Lima held a press conference in Rio de Janeiro where he made public the results of the twenty-volume, 5,115-page Figueiredo Report.[15]

According to one reporter who attended the press conference, the Figueiredo Commission had "found evidence of widespread corruption and sadism, ranging from the massacre of whole tribes by dynamite, machine guns and sugar laced with arsenic to the removal of an 11-year-old girl from school to serve as a slave to an

official of the Service." This same reporter noted that of 700 employees of the SPI, 134 were charged with crimes, 200 had been
dismissed, and another 38 who had been hired fraudulently had
been relieved of their duties.[16]

Following the press conference, a number of foreign observers
went to Brazil to investigate the situation revealed in the
Figueiredo Report, although rumors existed that the report had
been archived and then lost. One of these observers was Patrick
Braun, medical attaché to the French Department of Overseas
Territories, whose findings were reported in a *Medical Tribune
and Medical News* (New York) article, titled "Germ Warfare
Against Indians is Charged in Brazil." This article reported that
Braun had seen voluminous records that were previously un-
disclosed outside Brazil. Among the records he examined were
the files of the Brazilian ministries of Agriculture and the Interior
and the 5,115-page Figueiredo Report.

Brazilian government files, Braun was cited as saying, contained evidence that substantiated charges that Indian agents and
landowners had used biological as well as conventional weapons
to wipe out Indian tribes. These files indicated that outsiders had
deliberately introduced smallpox, influenza, tuberculosis, and
measles organisms among the tribes of the Mato Grosso region
between 1957 and 1963. In addition, the files of the Brazilian
minister of the interior also suggested that outsiders had con-
sciously introduced tuberculosis organisms among the tribes of
the northern section of the Amazon Basin in 1964 and 1965.
Braun told of evidence that he saw indicating that infectious organisms "were deliberately brought into Indian territories by
landowners and speculators utilizing a mestizo previously infected." Without immunity against these introduced diseases,
Braun was quoted as saying, countless Indians rapidly died.[17]

Another foreign observer who went to Brazil to investigate
these charges was a British journalist, Norman Lewis. In February 1969, Lewis published an article in the *Sunday Times* of London, titled "Genocide – From Fire and Sword to Arsenic and

Bullets, Civilization Has Sent Six Million Indians to Extinction." Lewis's article traced the history of Indian–white relations in Brazil and provided evidence indicating that the Indian Protection Service was a major accomplice in several crimes against Indians.

According to Lewis, over 100 Indian agents, including two of the recent directors of the SPI, had joined with frontier landowners and speculators in the systematic robbery and murder of Indians. Lewis noted that Major Luis Neves, the former head of the SPI, had been accused of forty-two crimes, including complicity in several murders, the robbery and illegal sale of Indian lands, and the embezzlement of $300,000. "It is not only through the embezzlement of funds," Lewis quoted Attorney General Figueiredo as saying, "but by the admission of sexual perversions, murders, and all other crimes listed in the penal code against Indians and their property, that one can see that the Indian Protection Service was for years a den of corruption and indiscriminate killings."[18]

The reports by Braun and Lewis, as well as several statements by anthropologists and scientific societies, were a major source of embarrassment for the new military government of Brazil and produced a momentary wave of protest throughout the world. A number of newspapers, for example, accused the Brazilian government of condoning a policy of genocide against its remaining Indian tribes and called for an immediate investigation by the United Nations. Even one of Brazil's most important newspapers, the *Jornal do Brasil*, had the courage to write, "The Indian Protection Service investigation will wind up in the United Nations. The crime is genocide and violations of the rights of man. It is better that crimes like this be exposed so that our shame may be seen in daylight."[19]

To this day it remains uncertain why the Brazilian government made public the findings of the highly controversial Figueiredo Report. One of the major reasons may have been the important role that General Albuquerque Lima played in Brazilian politics at this time. As minister of the interior, Albuquerque Lima attempted to unify various nationalist sectors in the Brazilian military. During his term of office, he not only called for a major investigation of Brazilian Indian policy, but also supported a parliamentary investigation of foreign penetration of the lands of the Amazon Basin. In addition, he favored a better distribution of income among the various regions of Brazil and approved of several protectionist economic policies voiced by nationalist elements in Brazil.[20]

In response to the findings of the Figueiredo Commission, General Albuquerque Lima did three things. First, he disbanded the Indian Protection Service and called for the establishment of a new government agency to be called the National Indian Foundation (FUNAI). Second, he promised that all criminals involved in the SPI scandal would be punished and that lands illegally sold or taken from Indians would be returned. And, finally, he invited several international organizations, such as the International Red Cross, to send fact-gathering missions to Brazil to witness Indian conditions with their own eyes.[21]

All these measures tended to weaken international protest concerning Brazilian Indian policy and no investigation of the Brazilian government was forthcoming from the United Nations. Then, in 1969, three events occurred that were to have important implications for the fate of the remaining Indian tribes of Brazil. The first event was the death of Brazilian President Arthur Costa e Silva and his replacement by General Emílio Garrastazú Médici. The second event was the disappearance of General Albuquerque Lima from Brazilian politics and his replacement in the office of minister of the interior by José Costa Cavalcanti. The third event was the announcement by the new Brazilian government that it was planning to invest over $500 million in the building of a transcontinental highway across the Amazon Basin.

The building of a highway system across the immense, but still unexplored, Amazon Basin had been a dream of Brazilian planners since the regime of President Getúlio Vargas in the

1930s. In June 1970, just months after assuming office as the new president of Brazil, General Médici turned this dream into a reality. "The initial problem of the Amazon," President Médici said at the time of the inauguration of construction on the Trans-Amazon Highway, "is to really get to know it. To do so, it is vital to make it more accessible and more open. Thus the policy of my government is directed primarily to the undertaking of a gigantic integration program with the two-fold objective of exploration and settlement."[22]

The building of the Trans-Amazon Highway had important repercussions on the nature of international attention that focused upon the situation of Indian tribes in Brazil. Almost overnight, it was the economic development of the Amazon Basin, rather than the threat to Brazilian Indians, that began to fill the pages of the international press.

Indians and the "Miracle"

Most foreign journalists looked upon the plan for the construction of the Trans-Amazon Highway and its consequent development programs as one part of the highly acclaimed "economic miracle" in Brazil. A 1971 article in the *New York Times*, for example, termed the Trans-Amazon Highway a "huge project to fit a big country." This article described Brazil as the "giant of Latin America." It said that Brazil had "made new economic strides" in the previous year by "shattering all statistical records in business and industry." The Trans-Amazon Highway, according to this article, was another "giant step," a highway that would "open up one of the last untapped areas of the world" and "add to Brazilian economic resources."[23]

Although the Brazilian "economic miracle" was in the making for several years, it did not actually come to world attention until 1968. From 1965 to 1968, for instance, gross domestic production in Brazil (the most undifferentiated but usual indicator of economic growth) reached a healthy 6 percent per year. Between

1968 and 1972, this indicator jumped to an exceptional 10 per-cent, and, in 1972, the rate of real economic growth reached 11.3 percent. According to the standard economic indicator, by this date Brazil was one of the top economic performers in the capitalist world.[24]

A similar pattern of growth occurred in exports from Brazil. Backed up by a substantial reduction in the rate of inflation, in 1971 exports totaled $3 billion (American billion). By 1973, this figure more than doubled, sending Brazil's export performance to more than $6 billion per year. Planners in Brazil pointed out that it took their country just two years (1971 to 1973) to achieve the same export record as Japan had taken six years (1958 to 1964) to produce. "While exports of many countries rose sharply during the 1973 economic boom," *Business Week* commented, "Brazil-ian exports positively exploded."[25]

This phenomenal economic performance led a number of foreign observers to point to Brazil as a classic case of the "free enterprise" model of capitalist development. At the height of the enthusiasm for the Brazilian "economic miracle," for example, the Business International Corporation (BIC) published a report, titled *Brazil: New Business Power in Latin America.* The BIC report noted that Brazil was at a "pivotal stage of its develop-ment." For centuries the country had been called the "sleeping giant of the Americas," but at the beginning of the decade of the 1970s it was finally "awake and stretching." According to BIC, Brazil had a "solid and varied industrial base" and was now "gear-ing up for that second stage of industrialization." This new phase of industrial growth, the BIC report claimed, would make Brazil "competitive in world markets, and possibly by the end of the de-cade of the 70s, make it a serious economic power by global stan-dards."[26]

Despite the essentially economic character of these reports, it would be misleading to claim that following 1970 there were no longer international news reports about the situation of Brazilian Indian tribes. The Trans-Amazon road system was a major ingredient in the Brazilian "economic miracle," and it cut through one of the most densely populated Indian areas of Brazil. Several of the articles that dealt with this road system also discussed the threat that the construction of this highway system posed to the Indian tribes along its path. Most of these articles, however, were superficial and tended to focus upon bloody skirmishes between highway workers and Indian tribes. As would be expected, Brazil was on the move, and for reporters in countries such as the United States it contained all the mystery, fantasy, and bloodshed of the most dramatic episodes out of the American West.[27]

A more comprehensive treatment of the situation of Indian tribes along the new Amazon roads was provided by the European press and by several international organizations who sent fact-gathering commissions to Brazil. In 1970, the first of these commissions, a three-member team from the International Red Cross, visited the interior regions of Brazil. Following this, in 1971, Robin Hanbury-Tenison carried out a study for the Primitive People's Fund/Survival International of London. Finally, in the summer of 1972, a four-member team from the Aborigines Protection Society (APS) of London, composed of Edwin Brooks, René Fuerst, John Hemming, and Francis Huxley, visited the Amazon region. The APS team wrote up their findings in several articles and a book, *Tribes of the Amazon Basin in Brazil, 1972.* Their report has since served as the basis of the European public's understanding of the contemporary situation of Indian peoples in Brazil.[28]

All these reports contain a vast amount of information and provide a good basis for evaluating the nature of the reformed Indian policy of FUNAI. In at least two areas, however, the reports are deficient. First, no report relates Brazilian Indian policy to the larger economic development policies of the Brazilian military regime. And, second, all the reports fail to provide a systematic analysis of the numerous ways in which international factors, emanating from Brazil's dependency on the world political economy, are contributing to the uprooting and demise of Amazonian Indian tribes.

A central contention of the present book is that in order to comprehend the situation of Brazilian Indians, it is necessary to examine the economic history of the Amazon region and to discuss the recent growth in the political economy of Brazil. Most of the factual reports cited above, I believe, have overemphasized the bureaucratic blunders of national Indian policies in Brazil, and have failed to analyze the relationships that exist between these policies and the more global "development strategy" for the occupation of the Amazon Basin. One of the main purposes of this book is to demonstrate how the present situation of Amazonian Indians, as well as that of several other social sectors, is closely related to the institutional factors that have brought about what a number of observers have termed the "economic miracle" in Brazil.

As early as 1957, Darcy Ribeiro argued for a political and economic perspective on the so-called Indian Problem in Brazil. "The fundamental determinant of the destiny of indigenous tribes, of the conservation or loss of their languages and cultures," Ribeiro wrote at this time, "is the national society or even the international economy."[29]

In another survey of Brazilian Indian policy published in 1962, Ribeiro claimed that:

Much more than the guarantees of the law, it is lack of economic interest which assures the Indian of the possession of the niche in which he lives. The discovery of anything which can be exploited is tantamount to the crack of doom for the Indians who are pressured to abandon their lands or slaughtered on them. And economic discoveries do not have to be exceptional for the Indians to be plundered.[30]

According to Ribeiro, these economic pressures were so great that the fate of even the most isolated, jungle-dwelling Indian tribes would be determined by small changes in Brazilian national society or market fluctuations in the world economy. "The quotation of rubber, nuts, and other products on the New York market, or the perspectives of peace or of war among the great powers," Ribeiro wrote, "influence the ebb or flow of the waves of extractors of forest products, permitting the last remaining autonomous tribes to survive or condemning them to extinction."[31]

In broad outlines, the present book is a further elaboration of the political and economic thesis contained in Darcy Ribeiro's early studies of Brazilian Indian policy. By way of background to this argument, however, it is necessary to do two things: first, to discuss the "development euphoria" that centered on the Brazilian Amazon during and following World War II; and second, to analyze several important institutional changes that have taken place in Brazil since the military coup of 1964. These topics, which will form the basis of my discussion of contemporary Indian policy in Brazil, are considered in the next two chapters.

Part one

The economic history of the Brazilian Amazon

1940 to 1970

2

Development plans in the postwar period

Nothing will stop us in this movement which is, in the 20th Century, the highest task of civilizing man: to conquer and dominate the valleys of the great equatorial torrents, transforming their blind force and their extraordinary fertility into disciplined energy. The Amazon, under the impact of our will and our labor, shall cease to be a simple chapter in the history of the world and, made equivalent to other great rivers, shall become a chapter in the history of civilization.

Getúlio Vargas, speech given at Manaus, October 1940

The first indication that the Brazilian government was planning to open up and develop the Amazon region appeared in 1940 when Getúlio Vargas, the great Brazilian populist and founder of the Estado Novo, traveled throughout the sparsely populated northern regions of Brazil. Vargas was the first Brazilian president to visit the Amazon and took advantage of the opportunity to confer with a number of recently contacted Indian tribes. On one occasion, he distributed machetes and hoes to Indians and took a canoe ride with local tribesmen. Photographers caught the dynamic Getúlio smoking a cigar with an Indian chief and recorded his presence at a special ceremony and dance. When Vargas returned to Rio de Janeiro, he went before the press, and announced that he had just approved a plan for the colonization of the distant State of Goiás; an enthusiastic government program that would provide settlers with a free house and fifty acres of public land.[1]

On October 5, 1940, Vargas returned to the Amazon. This

time his first stop was the huge Belterra Rubber Plantation, founded by Henry Ford in 1934, where Getúlio praised the "planned," "systematic," and "rational" ways in which the great American industrialist had exploited the Amazon's riches. Then, Vargas arrived in the city of Manaus, where the local upper classes held a banquet in his honor. In a speech following this banquet, Vargas proclaimed:

Everything which has up to now been done in Amazonas, whether in agriculture or extractive industry, has been an empirical realization, and must be transformed into rational exploitation. What nature offers us here is a magnificent gift, which demands the care and the cultivation of the hand of man. From (the regime of) sparse colonization, subservient to casual interests, consuming energy with but slight profit, we must change over to the concentration and fixation of the human element.

In the course of this speech, Vargas also told his audience that:

The impressive movement of national reconstruction substantiated in the establishment of the regime of November 10th (1937) could not overlook you because you are the land of the future, the valley of promise in the life of Brazil of tomorrow. Your definite entry in the economic life of the nation, as a factor of prosperity and creative energy will be accomplished without delay.[2]

Two days later, on October 7, Vargas went by airplane to Porto Velho, a city at the far western end of the Amazon Basin. Here, at an unexpected press interview, Vargas announced that he was about to call a special conference of countries that bordered on the Amazon to discuss mutual problems of trade, navigation, transport, and tariffs. Vargas told the Brazilian press that:

I have not come to the Amazon with the outlook of a tourist, who finds here so many reasons for astonishment and for carrying away profound impressions. I have come with the purpose of seeing to the practical possibilities of putting into execution a plan for the systematic exploitation of the wealth and the economic development of the great valley.

During this press interview, Vargas suggested that a cure for the economic backwardness of the Amazon would come through agrarian colonies, sytematic planning, scientific methods, and technical steps to improve the health conditions of the people in the basin. Most important, on this trip Vargas made it clear that he would invite representatives of the United States to any conference that would discuss the economic future of the Amazon countries. "Already to arrive," Vargas revealed, "are North American industrialists who are interested in collaborating with us in the development of Amazônia, where their capital and technical resources will find a secure and remunerative application."[3]

The conference of South American countries suggested in Getúlio Vargas's press interview at Porto Velho in October 1940 never did occur. Vargas's trip to the Amazon, however, marked a turning point in relations between Brazil and the United States. By late 1940, Brazilian diplomats were traveling to Washington to discuss an arms agreement for mutual defense. Then, in October 1941, the United States signed a Lend-Lease Agreement with Brazil that promised $100 million worth of future arms and discussed the possible stationing of American troops in the Northeast of Brazil. By 1942, the alliance between the two nations was complete. New negotiations at the highest levels of both governments raised the Lend-Lease Arms Agreement to $200 million and opened the way for American exploitation of the rich mineral resources of Brazil.[4]

From the point of view of the Amazon, the most important of these agreements were a $100 million U.S. Export-Import Bank loan to develop raw materials in Brazil and a $5 million contract between the Brazilian government and the U.S. Rubber Reserve Company for purposes of increasing rubber production in the Amazon. During the war, the Institute for Inter-American Affairs was created in Washington in order to coordinate activities between the United States and its South American allies. As one of its first acts, the institute sponsored a multimillion-dollar program of mineral exploration, public health, rubber growing, and food production in Brazil.[5]

Throughout the war years, geologists from the U.S. Geological Survey made studies of Brazilian resources in lead, zinc, talc, manganese, barite, and other strategic materials. By the end of the war, more than a dozen Geological Survey technicians were stationed in Brazil.[6]

World War II marked a new era in the economic history of the Amazon Basin. During the final years of the war, several North American writers called for a major program of economic development in the Amazon region of Brazil. One of these writers was Earl Parker Hanson, an engineer and geographer, who published a pamphlet, *The Amazon: A New Frontier?* (1944), under the auspices of the Foreign Policy Association in the United States. In this pamphlet, Hanson presented a case for the prospects of a new "pioneer rush" to the Amazon Basin in the postwar years. The importance of this document was that it presented a systematic argument for the development of the Amazon in the years immediately following the war. An appendix traced the history of relations between Brazil and the United States.[7]

In a survey of wartime expansion into the Amazon, Hanson noted that:

The days of ruthless colonial exploitation are over and the South American nations must now begin to take active steps toward the all-around development of the Amazon Basin.[8]

Such a program, Hanson pointed out, had already been proposed in the speech of Brazilian President Getúlio Vargas at Manaus in 1940, but a number of false prejudices and opinions blocked its fulfillment. Several writers, for example, claimed that the nature of soil fertility in the tropics was an impediment to the rational consideration of expansion into the Amazon region. Hanson noted that all generalizations about soil fertility or lack of it break down in the face of the large size of the Amazon Basin and the rich alluvial soils discovered along the banks of its rivers. "Nobody," he wrote in response to those writers who had highlighted the poor qualities of Amazon soils, "can at this time foretell what shape and direction any future development will take."[9]

A similar case, Hanson argued, could be made about the Indians of the region. During the war, a number of conflicts had occurred between rubber collectors and hostile Indian tribes. In his pamphlet, Hanson described how attacks by Makiritare Indians along the Ventuari River in the Orinoco region of Venezuela had held back rubber workers during the war. At the same time, however, Hanson noted that Indians did not prevent the colonization and development of the American West. Pointing to the case of Brazil, he wrote:

The South American Governments are fully aware that a realistic Indian policy, including protection of settlers, must be inevitably part of any development plan.[10]

In the end, Hanson claimed that it would be political and economic interests, rather than natural obstacles, that would determine the future course of economic developments in the Amazon Basin. Modern technology and rational planning, he suggested, could overcome the problems of tropical climate, poor soil fertility, miserable health and sanitation conditions, and hostile Indians. "Already," Hanson wrote, "the dream of Amazon development is taking firm root in some of the South American countries today."[11]

According to Hanson, several factors could bring about the fulfillment of this dream. One of these factors was the "Good Neighbor Policy" of the United States which, following the war, could provide the various South American countries with aid and technical assistance for the systematic development of the Amazon Basin. A second factor was the large amount of surplus capital that would be available for investment in the Amazon Basin following the war. A third factor was the growing interest military men were showing in the resources of the Amazon region.

In reference to capital available after the war for investment in the Amazon Basin, Hanson wrote:

Show an investor a chance to make an eventual profit from the opening up and colonization of new grazing lands, the construction of slaughter houses, refrigeration plants, steamers with refrigerated holds; show him a chance to make a profit by putting his money in rubber plantations that are encouraged by government policies, protected by tariffs, and made possible through new immigration policies, and he does not much care if these ventures are located in the Amazon Basin or elsewhere.[12]

Hanson noted that several American military leaders, who were preoccupied with issues of "hemispheric defense," were also interested in having sources of rubber and other essential industrial supplies closer to home than Asia. "No matter how the world may be adjusted after the war," he wrote, "the fact will remain that it is easier to protect lines of supply from the Amazon Basin than across the wide Pacific."[13]

Finally, Hanson argued, the Amazon Basin would assume a new geopolitical significance following the war. Until recently, he claimed, the "world has expanded in an east-west direction," but "before long it will start a vigorous expansion" toward the frontiers that exist in the north and the south. Indeed, Hanson wrote:

If post-war conditions demand the continuance of our present "hemisphere economic thinking" under which all of the Americas stand and grow together, it is much more likely that the end of the war will see a new pioneer rush into all the remaining frontiers, from Alaska to Patagonia.[14]

According to this writer, the Amazon Basin, with its phenomenal natural resources and its strategic position in hemispheric defense, would assume a critical position in postwar relations between Brazil and the United States. Like several other writers of his time, Earl Parker Hanson predicted that a major development effort would take place in the Amazon Basin in the years immediately following the war.[15]

Economic changes in the Amazon
following World War II

Earl Parker Hanson's pamphlet of 1944 and Getúlio Vargas's speech of 1940 demonstrated the general interest of both the United States and Brazil in developing the Amazon Basin after the war. In fact, however, it was not until several decades later that the predictions of Vargas and Hanson actually did come true. During the immediate postwar years, and throughout the decade of the 1950s, the Amazon Basin played a rather insignificant role in the overall economic development of Brazil. For the purposes of this book, however, three factors are important to note for their influence on the economy of the Amazon region in the years immediately following the war.

First, in 1942, Brazil and the United States signed a special bilateral agreement for the creation of a major public health and disease-control program in the Amazon Basin. This program was called the Special Service for Public Health (SESP). According to U.S. government documents, the purposes of the SESP program in Brazil were threefold. Militarily, the SESP program was to "improve the health conditions in strategic areas, particularly with relation to requirements of our armed forces and those of our American allies." Economically, it was to "make possible increased production of critical materials in areas where bad health conditions exist." Politically and psychologically, it was to "demonstrate in deeds as well as words the tangible benefits of democracy in action and to win active support of the civilian population."[16]

Between 1942 and 1960, the U.S. government provided $16.8 million to the SESP program. During this period, over 200 North American health technicians and advisers were assigned to Brazil.

The importance of the SESP program was that it began to transform the health and medical conditions of human populations in the Amazon Basin. For the first time, diseases such as malaria, yaws, filariasis, intestinal parasites, brucellosis, Chaga's disease, and trichinosis were brought under some degree of control. By 1948, the SESP program had constructed more than forty health centers and thirty-four secondary health posts in the Amazon Basin. At the same time, it constructed hospitals in Belém, Breves, Fortaleza, Manaus, and Santarém, and began a program for training Brazilian medical and public health personnel. In 1960, the SESP program was fully taken over by the Brazilian government, although some observers noted that it was significantly less effective and efficient than in the past.[17]

A second factor of major economic significance during the postwar period was the growth of aviation in Brazil. In 1945, for example, one author wrote:

The Brazilian Government is air minded to the fullest degree. . . . Every possible effort is being made to develop aviation, both as a military and civilian service. . . . Great activity in pilot training, hangar construction, airport building, and the manufacture of national planes all evidence [sic] to the fact that the Government realizes fully how important aviation is to the country, and that it intends to push this development as far as it can.[18]

The United States also provided technical assistance for the growth of aviation in Brazil. In 1940, for instance, the United States negotiated with the Brazilian government for the expansion of Panair do Brasil, a subsidiary of Pan American Airways. During the war, it continued with these efforts by supplying pilot training and airplanes to Brazil. In the postwar period, it carried out a more extensive program of sales and training with Brazil through a special Inter-Departmental Agency called the Cooperative Aviation Program.[19]

As part of this aviation effort, in 1943, the Brazilian government created the Central Brazil Foundation in order to open up the vast interior regions of the country. The Central Brazil Foundation worked closely with the Brazilian Air Force (FAB) and with the Indian Protective Service in Brazil. In the late 1940s, the foundation built a network of airstrips and access roads across the states of Mato Grosso and Goiás. These roads and airstrips marked the first penetration of the Amazon Basin by other than river routes. They formed part of what Brazilians called the "Great Diagonal," a vast air-and-road communications network that linked up the coastal cities of Rio de Janeiro and São Paulo with the immense hinterlands of central and northern Brazil.[20]

Finally, throughout the 1940s and 1950s, a steady stream of immigrants began to move into the central region of Brazil. In 1949, thousands of Brazilian pioneers were reported to be immigrating to the wilderness areas surrounding the Tocantins and Upper Xingu rivers. Twenty-six regularly scheduled flights were landing in the frontier town of Anápolis, Goiás, every week. Fifty-thousand Brazilians were reported to be passing through this region every year on their way to "booming communities" that could not be found on maps before the war.[21]

During the 1950s, this wave of internal migration continued to increase. In the latter part of the decade, the construction of the new national capital at Brasília was completed. At the same time, construction began on the overland Belém–Brasília Highway. By 1960, the states of Mato Grosso, Goiás, and Pará were among the major agricultural and cattle-raising areas of Brazil. This internal migration, however, mainly occurred in central Brazil, and, in the early 1960s, still had not affected the much larger Amazon region to the west.[22]

In 1962, Charles Wagley of Columbia University returned to a town in the Amazon Basin that he had studied in 1948. In his earlier writings on the town, Wagley had expressed the hope that "a period of rapid social and economic change was imminent for the Amazon Valley." In 1962, Wagley found that this hope had still not come true. In the second edition of his book, *Amazon Town: A Study of Man in the Tropics*, he wrote:

The Amazon region of Brazil is not stagnant economically or socially. It has changed since 1948, but not as much as the rest of Brazil. The economy is still based upon extractive industries. The social and economic classes . . . are still basically the same. Communications remain inadequate; there have been no marked improvements in the fluvial transportation system since 1950. Roads, except in the vicinity of Belém and Manaus, have hardly been extended. Men still occupy the riverine areas of Amazonia.[23]

Two important factors appear to explain the relative lack of economic development in the Amazon Basin in the decades immediately following the war. First, as Wagley notes, during the postwar period the Brazilian government placed major emphasis upon economic development programs in other areas of Brazil. During this period, the national government undertook to develop industry in Rio de Janeiro and São Paulo. It constructed huge hydroelectric projects in the Northeast and Minas Gerais. It built transportation lines from urban centers to the new coffee lands in Southern Brazil. It promoted the construction of the new federal capital at Brasília in the State of Goiás. "The surge of interest in Amazonia during World War II and just afterwards smouldered," Wagley writes, "and the attention of the nation turned elsewhere."[24]

Second, during the postwar period, the Brazilian government maintained a protectionist attitude toward foreign companies who were interested in exploiting the rich natural resources of Brazil. An important example of such protectionism was the Brazilian government's policy toward foreign oil companies who wanted to gain control of the rich petroleum resources of the Amazon Basin.

As far back as the 1920s, several powerful companies had tried to gain rights to carry out oil explorations in the Amazon region of Brazil. In 1938, the Brazilian government responded to these encroachments by establishing the National Petroleum Council. The government hoped that this council would limit foreign penetration of the Amazon and eventually lead to the nationalization of all oil reserves in Brazil.

During World War II, it was uncertain whether Brazil would follow in the direction of the 1930s, by nationalizing the entire petroleum industry, or whether it would succumb to the influence and pressures of foreign firms. In 1940, for example, the Standard Oil Company of Brazil proposed a partnership between foreign capital and the national government for the exploration of oil in Brazil. Then, in 1947, a major political campaign emerged in Brazil for the establishment of a national oil industry. The slogan during this period, which formed the basis of Getúlio Vargas's electoral campaign in 1950, was "*O petroleo é nosso*" ("The petroleum is ours").

In 1953, Getúlio Vargas introduced legislation for the establishment of Petrobrás, the state-owned oil company in Brazil. Throughout the 1950s, Petrobrás was the major symbol of economic nationalism in Brazil. In the short space of seven years, the petroleum reserves of Brazil increased from 22 million to 600 million barrels. By 1960, Petrobrás produced over 45 percent of the oil consumed in Brazil. At the same time, it began to build several new oil refineries and to acquire tankers in order to augment its fleet.[25]

The establishment of Petrobrás was an extremely important element in postwar developments in the Amazon Basin. In contrast to Peru and Ecuador, Brazil refused to let foreign companies explore for oil in the Amazon Basin in the postwar years. During this period, the Brazilian government was willing to let the Amazon Basin remain economically backward and underdeveloped, rather than allow it to come under the influence of foreign firms. As will be shown in the following chapter, the position of the Brazilian government in relation to foreign investment in natural resources changed radically following the military coup of 1964. After several decades of nationalist struggle, the government reversed its position on foreign investment in the Amazon and set the groundwork for the penetration of foreign capital into the rich petroleum and mineral resources of Brazil.

3

The significance of the military coup of 1964

The Amazon region represents a twentieth of the area of this planet, a fifth of its water, and a third of its forests. The importance of the Amazon jungle is decisive, above all for Brazil. Not so much for its present economic role – at the moment, it is contributing less than 4 percent to the Brazilian Gross National Product – but for its potential wealth: it has 79.7 percent of the country's lumber reserves, 81 percent of its fresh water, half of its iron ore deposits, nearly 100 percent of its tin deposits, 93 percent of its aluminum, and the largest deposit of rock salt in the world, estimated at ten billion [American] tons. The Amazon region also possesses what is thought to be the largest oil deposit in the world. . . .

It is only recently, however, that effective measures have been taken to open up this great treasure-house, with the [Brazilian] Federal Government's decision to take real steps towards the occupation and "conquest" of the region. Up to very recently, the problems and difficulties of the Amazon area, while discussed at length, were never really faced, in any concrete way, by the succeeding governments. But some of the world's largest companies, particularly in the fields of mining, lumbering, and cattle-rearing, got to the actual work, confident that the projects would be highly profitable.

"The Amazon: Its Treasures Are Being Revealed," in *Brazilian Trends: Economic Development in Brazil* (1972)

The Brazilian military coup of April 1964, which replaced the regime of Brazilian President João Goulart with a group of generals and which has remained in power since that date, was an economic turning point for both Brazil and the Amazon Basin. In the years immediately following the coup, the military government introduced a series of new development policies that transformed the entire political economy of Brazil. Just eight years

32

after the military coup, for example, the well-known Brazilian economist Celso Furtado could write that Brazil was "engendering a new form of capitalism." During this period, several events occurred that indicated that the new military government was finally ready to accept the challenge of the Amazon and provide the needed state inputs to fulfill the dream Getúlio Vargas first articulated in his speech at Manaus in 1940. For the purposes of this book, four of these events are important to note.[1]

The first of these events was a series of sudden encroachments on Brazil's relatively nationalist mineral codes of 1934 and 1954. The Brazilian Mineral Code of 1934, like the petroleum legislation discussed in the previous chapter, contained a series of principles that reflected the interest of previous governments in maintaining state control over the rich mineral resources of Brazil. One of these principles separated the ownership of soil rights to land from the ownership and control of subsoil wealth. A second principle stated that the industrial exploitation of minerals could only be carried out under licenses from the federal government. A third principle stated that these licenses could only be granted to Brazilians or to firms that were organized and registered in Brazil.

All these principles were restated in the Brazilian Mineral Code of 1954. Following the passage of this code, several congressional commissions were set up to investigate the degree of foreign control over the iron ore, manganese, and bauxite resources of Brazil.[2]

The Hanna Mining Company of Cleveland, Ohio, was one of the major foreign companies to suffer from these legal restrictions. In 1956, Hanna purchased stock on the London Stock Exchange in a British-owned gold-mining company in Brazil called Saint John D'el Rey. This company was never profitable, but Hanna took advantage of its controlling stock to explore for iron ore in Minas Gerais. Under Hanna's direction, a series of new corporate arrangements were worked out that included a Brazilian subsidiary of Saint John D'el Rey, Companhia de Mineracão Novalimense, and a new company called Aguas Claras. In the late 1950s, Aguas Claras applied to the Ministry of Mines for authorization to handle all operations from the digging of ore to the loading of it on deep-water vessels.

During the early 1960s, the Brazilian government raised a series of questions about the legal propriety of Hanna's activities in Brazil. In 1961, Brazilian President Jânio Quadros initiated an investigation that challenged Hanna's legal rights to mine iron ore. In 1962, the new Brazilian President João Goulart used the results of this investigation as the basis for an expropriation decree.[3]

The military coup of 1964 reversed all these trends and opened the way for the expansion of the Hanna Mining Company in Brazil. In April 1965, just a year after the military coup, *Fortune* magazine wrote that "For Hanna, the revolt which overthrew Goulart . . . arrived like a last minute rescue by the First Cavalry." Whether Hanna Mining Company brought influence to bear on the events of April 1964 is still unknown. What is certain is that Hanna, along with several other multinational companies, directly benefited from new mining policies that were instituted in the years immediately following the coup.[4]

In the first two years of the new military regime, two important decisions were made that assured Hanna's presence in Brazil. The first of these was a presidential decree promulgated by Marshal Castelo Branco in December 1964. He reversed the Goulart administration's attempts to create a government monopoly over minerals in Brazil and endorsed the rights of private companies to exploit Brazil's rich iron ore reserves. The second decision, passed by the Brazilian Federal Court of Appeals in June 1966, gave Hanna the right to exploit its long-idle iron ore deposits in Minas Gerais.[5]

Both these decisions were extremely important in the growth of Hanna Mining Company in Brazil. In the late 1960s, Hanna joined with one of Brazil's largest private companies, Cia. Auxiliar de Empresas de Mineração (CAEMI), to form a new iron ore company called Minerações Brasileiras Reunidas (MBR). At the same time, Hanna extended its influence over the rapidly growing petrochemicals industry in Brazil through the purchase of a 14 percent interest in the Unipar Company, and began to enter the lucrative Brazilian bauxite sector through a joint venture with the Aluminum Company of America.[6]

Through a series of contacts with powerful Brazilian bankers, industrialists, and government officials, Hanna Mining Company slowly became one of the major multinational corporations in Brazil. In the rich iron ore triangle of Minas Gerais, it was followed by several other international mining companies. Among these companies were: Samitri, controlled by the Luxembourg Burbach-Eich-Dudelang Steel Company; Samarco, a joint venture controlled by Marcona International; and Ferteco Mineração, a company in which the German Thyssen group had a controlling interest.[7]

Meanwhile, as all these new multinational mining ventures were being formed in southern Brazil, another major mining boom was taking place in the Amazon Basin of Brazil. The U.S. Steel Corporation, which had had a mining subsidiary in Brazil since the early 1920s and which had provided technical assistance for the establishment of the Brazilian steel industry during World War II, played a major role in opening up this new mining frontier.[8]

In 1967, geologists from U.S. Steel discovered an immense 160,000-hectare (a hectare equals 2.47 acres) iron ore deposit in the Serra dos Carajas region of the state of Pará. At this time, Brazilian mining legislation authorized a maximum of only one 5,000-hectare concession per company. According to trade journal reports, U.S. Steel attempted to get around this legislation by taking out one concession in the name of its Brazilian subsidiary and by registering thirty-one additional concessions in the names of several of its directors and employees. The Brazilian minister of mines granted U.S. Steel its first concession, but held up a decision on the others for nearly two years. Then, in 1969, U.S.

Steel announced that it was forming a new joint venture with the state-owned mining company, Companhia Vale do Rio Doce (CVRD), in order to mine its Serra dos Carajas reserves.[9]

Following the announcement of this joint venture, the Brazilian government again changed its mineral legislation. Under this new legislation, a single company was able to hold rights to 50,000 hectares of land and could register an additional 30,000 hectares in the names of other subsidiaries. This new legislation had a major effect on mineral exploration activities in the Amazon Basin. For the first time since World War II, the Brazilian government began to actively promote, rather than set limits upon, foreign investment in the rich mineral resources of Brazil. As a result of such promotion, the annual rate of mineral claims requested from the Brazilian government jumped from 2,000 in 1968 to over 20,000 in 1975.[10]

A second important event in the years following the military coup was the introduction of a series of fiscal and tax incentives for the promotion of cattle-raising and agribusiness projects in the Amazon Basin. As mentioned in the previous chapter, throughout the 1950s a major wave of internal migration occurred in the central regions of Brazil. During the late 1960s, large cattle ranchers began to dominate this agricultural frontier. By 1966, over 1,000 private developers had established cattle ranches to the east and west of the Belém–Brasília Highway.

The capital, management, and technology for these new agribusiness projects came from rich Brazilian capitalists from the states of São Paulo and Minas Gerais. One of the largest farms in the region, for example, was the Suiá-Missú Ranch, owned by Orlando Ometo, a wealthy sugar producer from São Paulo State. The Suiá-Missú Ranch covered nearly 5,000 square miles and was as big as the State of Connecticut in the United States. In just two years of operation, Orlando Ometo cleared 144,000 acres of land, built a 60-mile access road, and began to graze more than 15,000 head of cattle on his ranch.[11]

In October 1966, a major boost was given to this new cattle

frontier when the Superintendency for the Development of the Amazon (SUDAM) announced the creation of a far-reaching fiscal and tax-incentives program to promote more corporate farms in the Amazon Basin. The purpose of the SUDAM tax-incentives program was to mobilize companies in São Paulo and other parts of Brazil to reinvest their taxable incomes in cattle-raising projects in the Amazon. One part of this legislation provided that companies established in the Amazon before the end of December 1974, and considered to be of regional economic interest by SUDAM, would be exempt from all taxes for a period of ten years. A second provision granted companies a 50 percent reduction on their corporate income taxes earned in other parts of Brazil if they reinvested taxable monies in the Amazon. Finally, a third part of this legislation provided that the purchase of all farm machinery would be exempt from import taxes and duties.[12]

Within the next decade, SUDAM hoped that over 500 large cattle ranches would be established under this program in the Amazon and central regions of Brazil. One of the first companies to take advantage of the new program was the famous King Ranch of Texas. In 1968, King Ranch, in collaboration with the combined Swift-Armour Company of Brazil, was granted authorization to establish a 180,000-acre cattle ranch in a place called Paragominas, State of Pará. According to executives of the company, the objectives of the King Ranch project were to prove that cattle-breeding and range-and-grass technology practices used in Texas, Australia, and New Zealand could be transferred, with only slight modifications, to the tropical wetlands of Pará. Following King Ranch, several other foreign companies established agribusiness projects in the Amazon.[13]

The third event occurred in December 1966 and indicated that the Brazilian government was about to transform the entire regional economic picture in Brazil. At that time, Brazilian President Marshal Castelo Branco called together over 300 top government officials, planners, and businessmen for a conference to discuss the economic future of the Amazon Basin. This conference was held aboard a 10,451-ton ocean liner called the *Rosa da Fonseca* and had all the pomp and excitement of Getúlio Vargas's trip to the Amazon in 1940. During the course of the week-long cruise, experts and businessmen from Brazil, the United States, Mexico, Peru, and Germany discussed over fifty projects in the fields of cattle raising, agriculture, fibers, sugar, rice, oilseed, and timber production. Finally, the *Rosa da Fonseca* landed in the city of Manaus, and Castelo Branco announced "Operation Amazon" – a special five-year government program that would spend nearly $2 billion (American billion) on the development of transport, power, communications, and natural resources in the Amazon Basin.[14]

The announcement of "Operation Amazon" was an extremely important event in the opening up of the Brazilian Amazon. By the late 1960s, it was clear that the Brazilian government was interested in an integral rather than a piecemeal approach to the development of the Amazon Basin. "Brazil," a prominent government minister declared in 1967, "has resolved to accept the Amazon challenge and is going to occupy and exploit the area."[15]

It was a short step from the announcement of "Operation Amazon" in 1966 to the final event in the opening up of the Amazon Basin, the announcement of the famous Plan for National Integration in 1970. Actually, the precipitative event for this new program was a devastating drought that struck the northeastern region of Brazil in the spring of that year. At the time of this drought, the newly instated president of Brazil, General Emílio Garrastazú Médici, visited the Northeast and was reported to have been "deeply moved" by the sight of thousands of famished refugees seeking work and food along the roads.

In the days immediately following his visit, President Médici revealed that the Brazilian government was planning to construct the Trans-Amazon Highway. The new highway, according to Médici, would serve to resolve the agrarian problems of the

Northeast and carry the landless population of that region to the unpopulated lands of the Amazon. "Men without land in the Northeast," Médici told the Brazilian press, "Land without men in the Amazon."[16]

On paper, the Brazilian government's plan for the colonization of the Amazon was an impressive one. According to the plan, a 100-kilometer stretch of land on each side of the new Trans-Amazon Highway would remain as part of the public domain and be distributed, under a well-financed state program, to settlers from the Northeast. The new program would be directed by the Brazilian Institute for Agrarian Reform and Colonization (INCRA). By 1980, INCRA officials hoped, more than 5 million people would be relocated under this program along the margins of the new Trans-Amazon Highway.[17]

Several reports compared the INCRA colonization program to the Homestead Act legislation in the United States. Every 6 miles along the road, for example, INCRA planned to construct an *agrivillage* serving groups of from forty-eight to sixty families. Twenty-two such agrivillages within a radius of 30 miles would constitute an *agrópolis*. Three of these agrópolises would form a *rurópolis*, an urban center of more intense industrial and commercial activities in the Amazon. As for the migrants themselves, each would receive four things from INCRA: a modest house with 5 acres of cleared land; at least 250 acres of land with provisional title making the peasant owner eligible to participate in a financing fund established by the Bank of Brazil and the Bank of the Northeast; a minimum wage for at least six months; and guaranteed prices for his agricultural production.[18]

The Brazilian government argued that the Trans-Amazon Highway and the INCRA colonization program would be critical factors in the overall economic development of Brazil. A study that was published by the Brazilian National Highway Department (DNER) at the time of the announcement of these programs, for example, claimed that the major benefit of these programs would be in easing the traditional regional economic imbalances of Brazil. According to this study, the Center-South of Brazil, where the large industrial metropolises of Rio de Janeiro and São Paulo are located, accounted for only 26 percent of Brazil's area, but contained 67 percent of the country's population and enjoyed 83 percent of the national income. In contrast, the Northeast covered 15 percent of the area of Brazil, but contained 25 percent of the population and enjoyed only 13 percent of the national income. Finally, there was the Amazon region, which covered 39 percent of Brazil's land area, but which presently contained only 8 percent of the population and enjoyed less than 4 percent of national income.

This study claimed that the new highway and colonization projects, like the building of the federal capital at Brasília in the late 1950s, would alleviate these regional imbalances and redirect the economic life of the country from the coastal regions and the Center-South to Brazil's immense northern frontier. Eventually, government planners argued, these programs would create the conditions for the economic integration of Brazil.[19]

At the inauguration of the new highway construction program in October 1970, President Médici said, "The Trans-Amazon Highway will be an open route to enable the inhabitants of the Northeast to colonize the vast demographic wasteland and start to utilize its hitherto inaccessible potential." During the next five years, the president revealed, the Brazilian government would spend over a billion dollars (American billion) in a massive program of highway building, rural resettlement, mineral exploration, and hydroelectric and port construction in the Amazon Basin. The new program, now called the Plan for National Integration (PIN), would replace "Operation Amazon" announced in 1966.[20]

Although some members of the military regime stressed the "security" consideration involved in PIN, for most the plan was seen as the first step in the eventual economic integration of the most backward and underdeveloped region of Brazil. In January 1973, for example, Brazilian Minister of Planning João Paulo dos

Reis Velloso published an article that described the Amazon program as bringing about a "dramatic transformation of society" in Brazil. It would include the opening up of the last "economic frontiers" of the country, and the development of an "economically tenuous area" covering over 2 million square miles of land. The federal government, Reis Velloso claimed, was spending $1.5 billion (American) a year on new technology to develop the resources of this area and taking into account the ecological balance of the region. Most important, he wrote:

Large contingents now engaged in simple subsistence activities will progressively enter the market economy through programs aimed at giving small, rural producers access to land.[21]

The policies introduced by the Brazilian government following 1970 began to transform the entire economic structure of the Amazon Basin. In order to understand the nature of these policies, two points are important to note. First, in order to finance its economic development programs, the government was forced to borrow large sums of money fron international lending institutions and foreign banks. Between the military coup of 1964 and June 1971, for example, the U.S. government and its various international lending institutions provided the Brazilian government with over $3.5 billion (American) in bilateral aid and international loans. In 1972, Brazil surpassed Japan as the largest borrower from the U.S. Export-Import Bank and was the major debtor nation to the World Bank.[22]

During this period, the Brazilian government also borrowed heavily from private foreign banks. A 1970 study by the Economic Commission on Latin America (ECLA), for example, indicated that the yearly rate of increase of medium- and long-term loans to Brazil tripled between 1965 and 1969. By this time, the annual rate of short-term liabilities of Brazil increased over eightfold, reaching a level of $388 million in 1969.[23]

Second, at the time of the announcement of the Plan for National Integration, foreign and multinational corporations controlled the command posts of the Brazilian economy. Foreign control of the upper levels of the Brazilian economy increased significantly throughout the 1960s. A study done in 1962, for example, found that twenty-nine of the fifty-five largest "economic groups" in Brazil were foreign controlled and that most groups controlled by Brazilians had close ties to foreign firms.[24]

By the late 1960s, Brazil's major business magazine reported that two-thirds of the fifty largest firms in its "Top 500 Brazilian Firms" were foreign subsidiaries. In 1969, 90 percent of the automobile industry in Brazil, 87 percent of pharmaceuticals, 73 percent of heavy machinery, 65 percent of chemicals and plastics, and 33 percent of the steel industry were in foreign hands.[25]

More recent data for the early 1970s provide a similar picture. A study using information from 1972 found that American and other foreign firms accounted for 158 of the 500 largest nonfinancial enterprises in Brazil. In the manufacturing sector, these foreign corporations accounted for 147 of the 300 largest firms and 59 of the 100 largest firms. "MNC [multinational corporation] conduct," this report stated, "is a critical determinant of Brazilian economic performance. If denationalization and product market concentration continue to rise, the Brazilian economy will find itself increasingly vulnerable to the power of foreign decision-makers in the home offices of multinational corporations."[26]

Over the past decade, a new partnership has emerged in Brazil between international lending institutions, multinational corporations, and the Brazilian military regime. The strength of this partnership has been a primary factor in the rapid opening up of the Brazilian Amazon. In the next sections of this book, I shall assess what this partnership has meant for the Indian tribes of the Amazon Basin. One of my main purposes will be to demonstrate the several ways in which contemporary Indian policy has become institutionally compromised with the wider economic development policies of the Brazilian military regime. By way of introduction to this discussion, however, it is necessary to retrace our historical narrative and discuss the significance of the important Indianist experiment created by Orlando, Claudio, and Leonardo Villas Boas in the Xingu National Park.

Part two

Contemporary Indian policy in Brazil

1970 to 1975

4

The Villas Boas brothers and Indian policy in Brazil

All my work as a doctor among the Indians of Brazil was oriented to a single idea: that the rapid process of civilizing the Indian is the most effective form of killing him.

> Dr. Noel Nutels, Brazilian Indianist with over twenty-five years of medical experience among Brazilian tribes

We are exterminating the Indian, and doing so in the worst possible way – by convincing ourselves that we are great humanists, extending over the Indian wings of protection. But what kind of protection can we really offer him? Perhaps what we are really interested in is the little bit of land the Indian still possesses. Or, perhaps we are seeking a source of cheap labor. This is how you can interpret all the humanity we have been imposing on the Indian.

> Orlando Villas Boas, former Director of the Xingu National Park, Mato Grosso, Brazil

When the Brazilian National Indian Foundation (FUNAI) was created in 1967, two opposing models of Indian policy existed in Brazil. One of these models, which was radically protectionist in nature, was developed by Orlando, Claudio, and Leonardo Villas Boas in the Xingu National Park. According to this model, Indian tribes should be protected by the federal government from frontier encroachments in closed Indian parks and reserves, and be prepared gradually, as independent ethnic groups, to integrate into the wider society and economy of Brazil. In opposition to the Villas Boas brothers' philosophy was a second model of Indian policy that was developed by the Brazilian Indian Protection Service in the final years of its existence and later assumed by FUNAI. This model was developmentalist in nature and was based on the premise that Indian groups should be rapidly integrated, as a reserve labor force or as producers of marketable commodities, into the expanding regional economies and rural class structures of Brazil. The significance of these two models for contemporary Indian policy in Brazil will be explored in this chapter. To begin, however, it is necessary to discuss the philosophy of the Villas Boas brothers and to describe the important Indianist experiment that they created in the Xingu National Park.[1]

The Villas Boas brothers and the Xingu National Park

Orlando (born 1914), Claudio (born 1916), and Leonardo (born 1918, died 1961) Villas Boas were sons of a middle-class Brazilian family from the State of São Paulo. In 1943, the three brothers joined the famous Roncador–Xingu Expedition to the unexplored regions of Central Brazil. At this time, Brazilian nationalists feared that one of the consequences of World War II would be a major movement of European settlers to the interior regions of Brazil. As a response to these fears, the government created the Roncador–Xingu Expedition. The Roncador–Xingu Expedition constructed a series of emergency airstrips between Manaus and southern Brazil. In 1944, the expedition made contact with the then-hostile Xavante tribe. In 1946, it reached the headwaters of the Xingu River and made peaceful contact with the numerous Indian tribes that occupied the Upper Xingu. Finally, in 1953, the expedition reached Manaus, establishing an air route between the northern and southern parts of Brazil.[2]

In a recent account of their early experiences, Orlando and Claudio Villas Boas note that in 1946 the Indian tribes of the Upper Xingu were living in almost the same conditions as those witnessed by the German ethnologist Karl von den Steinen in 1884. In 1946, there were more than a dozen distinct Indian tribes in the Xingu region, representing the four major aboriginal language families of Brazil (Tupi, Arawak, Carib, and Gê). In regard to conditions that existed in the Upper Xingu at this time, the Villas Boas brothers write:

The distribution of villages in the region was identical; the com-munication and the relations among them the same; the natives still displayed the same peaceful nature, the same hospitality and curiosity that is transformed on contact with strangers into the naïve and friendly attitude that so impressed the German explorer and inspired him to make a highly detailed and expressive record of them.[3]

According to the Villas Boas brothers, the only appreciable changes that had taken place in the Xingu region between 1884 and 1946 were a substantial reduction in the size of native groups and the introduction of a small number of metal tools. The brothers attribute the decrease in population to the first violent outbreaks of influenza, dysentery, and other infectious diseases that began to invade the region thirty years before. Apparently, at this time, groups of Indians inhabiting the lower Kurizêvo River began to travel upstream and made contact with Brazilian settlers along the Upper Paranatinga River, at the Simões Lopes Indian Post, and in other places. These tribes had traveled to the Brazil-ian settlements in order to acquire metal tools, and on their re-turn infected the other tribes of the region. "The Indians," the Villas Boas brothers write, "were completely defenseless against these diseases and practically all of them died. The few who managed to get back to their villages were carriers, and the devas-tation spread to an even larger number of defenseless people."[4]

As a result of these first experiences with the Indian tribes of the Upper Xingu, the Villas Boas brothers decided to remain in the region and to dedicate their lives to the Indians' welfare and protection. In consultation with the aging Rondon (who died in 1958) and his small remaining circle of dedicated Indianist col-laborators, the Villas Boas brothers began to reevaluate the his-tory and consequences of Indian policy in Brazil. The brothers found that the worst aspect of this policy was its tendency to make contact with Indian tribes only to find later that they were wiped out by more powerful economic interests along the Brazilian frontiers. Hence, the brothers decided that what was needed was a positive program of Indian protection – a program that would provide Indians both with a land base to continue their traditional modes of economic subsistence and with medical assistance against outside diseases.

The Villas Boas brothers further argued that it was the responsibility of the federal government to provide a secure protective buffer, in the form of closed Indian parks and reserves, between Indians and the frontiers of national society. In time, the three brothers believed, Indians would integrate into Brazilian national society. This process of integration, however, should be a gradual one and should guarantee the Indians' survival, ethnic identities, and ways of life.[5]

In 1952, this novel Indianist philosophy became a reality when the vice-president of Brazil called a round table to debate the creation of a national Indian park in the Upper Xingu Basin. At the time, conditions were ripe for such a discussion in Brazil. From 1950 to 1954, the Indian Protection Service (SPI) was headed by one of Brazil's most dedicated Indianists, José Maria da Gama Malcher. In addition, during this period there was a great deal of nationalist sentiment in Brazil and a feeling that a system of national parks would protect the natural and historical patrimony of the country.

On April 27, 1952, Brigadier Raimundo Vasconcelos Aboim, Heloisa Alberto Torres, Orlando Villas Boas, and Darcy Ribeiro submitted a legal document to the vice-president calling for the establishment of the Xingu National Park. This legal document petitioned the federal government to set aside a large area in the northern part of the State of Mato Grosso for the creation of Brazil's first Indian park. The park was to be an experiment of sorts in which Indian tribes and the natural habitats they occupied would be protected against the dangers of a society in the midst of rapid economic change. The Villas Boas brothers were named as the first directors of the park and it was placed under the joint responsibility of the SPI, the National Museum in Rio de Janeiro, the Osvaldo Cruz Institute, the National Research Council, and the Institute of History and Geography of Mato Grosso.[6]

In the years that followed, two major threats faced the Xingu National Park. The first threat was an attempt by the government of Mato Grosso to provide land concessions in the park to real estate companies and land speculators. An investigation carried out by the SPI in 1954 revealed that more than 6 million hectares of land had already been transferred in this manner and that title to over 75 percent of the area set aside for the park had passed into non-Indian hands. Through a press campaign mobilized by the Villas Boas brothers and a small group of employees of the SPI, the extent of this land encroachment was exposed, and the federal government placed pressure on the state government of Mato Grosso to nullify the titles it had previously granted. Fortunately, this rapid intervention by the federal government proved successful, and the territorial integrity of the Xingu National Park was at this time maintained.[7]

In the same year, however, a second and more critical threat occurred in the form of a measles epidemic that struck almost every tribe. This epidemic was so devastating and spread so rapidly that it almost wiped out all the already reduced tribes of the Upper Xingu Basin. Among the Kamayurá tribe, for example, 18 of 112 surviving members were killed by the 1954 epidemic; among the Awetí, 8 of 31; among the Waurá, 21 of 104; among the Kuikúru, 10 of 145; among the Kalapálo, 40 of 150; among the Trumái, 2 of 21. Most critical, this measles epidemic was so widespread (100 percent affected in most tribes) that Indians were unable to maintain their gardens and their hunting and fishing activities. Malnutrition and hunger complicated the spread of the disease.[8]

At the time of this outbreak, the Villas Boas brothers mobilized support from a group of doctors at the Medical School in São Paulo and from a team of public health officials associated with Dr. Noel Nutels in Rio de Janeiro. These medical personnel, in association with the Brazilian Air Force (FAB), rushed immediate aid to the region and fortunately were able to stop the measles epidemic before it destroyed all the tribes. Further, following this epidemic, the Villas Boas brothers organized a systematic program of public health, inoculations, and medical assistance for the Indians in the park. This program proved invaluable in controlling other epidemics that struck the Upper Xingu region in the 1950s and 1960s. By the early 1960s, in fact, almost all epidemic diseases (measles, Spanish influenza, pulmonary diseases introduced during earlier periods of contact, etc.) were brought under control, and the tribes of the Xingu were increasing in size.[9]

On April 19, 1961, the Brazilian Congress passed Decree No. 50.455, which established the legal boundaries of the Xingu National Park. According to Orlando and Claudio Villas Boas, in creating the Xingu National Park, the Brazilian government had two important goals in mind: (1) to build a natural reservation where flora and fauna would be safeguarded for the distant future of the country, as evidence of what Brazil was like at the time of discovery; and (2) to extend protection immediately to the indigenous tribes of the region, offering them assistance and defending them from premature and harmful contacts along the expanding frontiers of Brazilian society.[10]

In 1961, at the time of its official creation by the Brazilian Congress, there were fourteen tribes living in the Xingu National Park, divided into two major concentrations. In the southern part of the park, around the Leonardo Villas Boas Indian Post (formerly called Pôsto Capitão Vasconcelos) were ten tribes numbering approximately 700 people. These tribes included the Kamayurá and Awetí (Tupi); the Kuikúru, Kalapálo, Matipuhy, and Nafuquá (Carib); the Waurá, Mehináku, and Yawalapití (Arawak); and the Trumái, belonging to an isolated linguistic family.

In the northern part of the park, around the Diauarum Indian Post, were the Suyá and Txukahamae (Gê), the Kayabí (Tupi), and the Jurúna of uncertain linguistic affiliation.[11]

Recently a Brazilian anthropologist, Carmen Junqueira, has made an assessment of the effects of the Villas Boas brothers' policy on the Kamayurá tribes, who live in the southern part of the Xingu National Park. Junqueira notes that the implementation of a protectionist policy has entailed a "delicate interference" in the way of life of the Kamayurá and has brought about several unforeseen structural changes in the relationships of the tribe. Among the most important of these changes, Junqueira claims, is the great degree of economic dependency that has been created between the Kamayurá and Indian agents in the park.

For several years, the Villas Boas brothers supplied tribes such as the Kamayurá with a wide range of metal tools and material goods. As a result of this policy, several important changes took place in the relations within and between tribal groups. Among the most important of these changes were a decrease in native craft production, and a corresponding movement away from intertribal trade toward greater economic dependency on the Indian post. Another important change was a decrease in the power of native chiefs and a corresponding increase in the power of Indian post employees. Junqueira writes:

The Kamayurá did not escape being absorbed by Brazilian society. In order to subsist, the economy of the group became dependent upon the supply of goods produced by foreign agents. The power which used to lie in the hands of the indigenous chiefs became centralized and was displaced outside of the limits of the group.[12]

At the same time, however, Junqueira argues that these changes did not have any major "disruptive effects" on the Kamayurá tribe. During the period of her field research, the Kamayurá population was increasing in size. The Indians still maintained their ethnic identity apart from Brazilian society and were able to integrate culturally many of the new material items and ideas being disseminated from the Indian post. Most important, the productive system of the Kamayurá was the same as it was in the past. The new tools introduced into the tribe enabled the Kamayurá to increase the productivity of their traditional hunting, fishing, and gardening economies, and temporarily freed them from the necessity to participate more directly in the wider market economy and class structure of Brazil.

In general, Junqueira argues that the Xingu National Park, under the direction of the Villas Boas brothers, was a successful experiment in Indian protectionism. In the short run, she notes, the Villas Boas brothers were able to insure the survival of indigenous populations by adopting preventive health measures and by controlling all contacts between Indians and outsiders. In the long term, the Villas Boas brothers tried to convince the Indians to remain as an autonomous people for the day when they would come into more direct contact with Brazilian society. For this purpose, innovations were introduced slowly, while at the same time attempts were made to preserve the social cohesion in each of the tribal groups.

The Brazilian National Indian Foundation and the invasion of the Xingu National Park

When the Brazilian National Indian Foundation (FUNAI) was created in December 1967, it appeared as if the new agency might follow the experiences developed by the Villas Boas brothers in the Xingu National Park. At the time of the establishment of FUNAI, General Albuquerque Lima was the minister of the interior. As one of his first acts, Albuquerque Lima authorized the extension of the area of the Xingu National Park from 22,000 to 30,000 square kilometers. At the same time, the minister called for the establishment of a number of new Indian reserves (federally recognized land areas occupied by a single Indian tribe) and the creation of three new Indian parks: the Tumucumaque Indian Park in the extreme north of the State of

Table 1. *Brazilian Indian parks and reserves, 1972 (in square kilometers)*

Name	Approximate size	State or territory
National parks		
Araguaia	19,430	Goiás
Aripuanã	32,000	Mato Grosso/ Rondônia
Ituí (proposed)	n.d.	Amazonas
Tumucumaque	26,930	Pará
Xingu	21,600	Mato Grosso
Yanomamö (proposed)	22,700	Roraima
Indian reserves		
Apiaká	1,130	Mato Grosso
Areões	1,430	Mato Grosso
Aripaktsá	1,130	Mato Grosso
Couto Magalhães	620	Mato Grosso
Irántxe	n.d.	Mato Grosso
Kararão	n.d.	Pará
Karitiâna	n.d.	Rondônia
Parakanân	n.d.	Pará
Parecís	5,650	Mato Grosso
Pimentel Barbosa	620	Mato Grosso
Sangradouro	n.d.	Mato Grosso
São Marcos	n.d.	Mato Grosso
Tapayúna	10,250	Mato Grosso
Waimirí-Atroarí	n.d.	Amazonas
Xerente	n.d.	Goiás

Note: n.d. indicates no data available.
Sources: R. J. A. Goodland and Howard S. Irwin, *Amazon Jungle: Green Hell to Red Desert?* (Amsterdam, 1975), Tables 12, 13; and João Américo Peret, *População Indígena do Brasil* (Rio de Janeiro, 1975), Map 3.

Pará, the Aripuanã Indian Park in Rondônia and western Mato Grosso, and the Araguaia Indian Park on the Ilha do Bananal (see Table 1 for a listing of Indian parks and reserves in Brazil).[13]

In terms of formal policy, the reorganization of the Indian

bureau in Brazil seemed to be a step in the right direction. The first article of the statute establishing FUNAI, for example, included the following provisions:

1. respect for tribal institutions and communities;
2. guarantee of the permanent possession of lands that Indians inhabit, and the exclusive use of natural resources therein, according to the Brazilian Constitution;
3. preservation of the biological and cultural equilibrium of Indian communities in contact with national society; and
4. defense of the spontaneous acculturation of Indian communities, rather than their rapid and enforced acculturation.[14]

The above statute was approved on January 31, 1968, and amended on May 2, 1969. The provisions contained in this statute recognized the inadequacies of the former Indian Protection Service in Brazil and reflected the best aspects of the protectionist Indian policy developed by the Villas Boas brothers in the Xingu National Park. At the time of its passage, it appeared as if there might be a major change in the nature of Indian policy in Brazil.

In 1970, however, an important redirection took place in the administration and philosophy of FUNAI. In June of that year, a former military intelligence officer, General Oscar Jerônimo Bandeira de Mello, was named as the new president of FUNAI. On assuming office, Bandeira de Mello announced that Indian policy would be carried out within the framework of the overall Plan for National Integration in Brazil. The general claimed that FUNAI, as an agency within the Brazilian Ministry of the Interior, would provide protection to Indian tribes, but this protection would be coordinated with the more global program for the occupation and settlement of the Amazon. "Ethnic minorities, such as the Brazilian Indians," the general was quoted as saying in one of his first public speeches, "must be oriented to a well-defined planning process, taking into account their participation in national progress and integration as producers of goods."[15]

During his first year in office, Bandeira de Mello introduced two important measures to implement this new vision of Indian policy in the administration of FUNAI. The first of these measures was the reintroduction of the so-called *renda indígena*, or indigenous income, a special institution developed during the final years of the SPI. Throughout the late 1950s and the early 1960s, an entrepreneurial mentality characterized the outlook of many of the high officials in the SPI. During this period, the SPI converted several Indian posts into economic enterprises where Indians were forced to sell the products of their labor to Indian agents and where Indian lands and resources were leased to outsiders for mineral, timber, and grazing rights. At the same time, the SPI created a special fund, called the indigenous income, which represented the income from Indian lands and which became a means of paying the salaries of Indian agents and alleviating the costs of Indian affairs. These economic practices were criticized in the Figueiredo Report of 1968, and were a major reason for the demoralization and collapse of the SPI.[16]

In 1970, General Bandeira de Mello supported the reintroduction of the indigenous income fund into the administration of FUNAI. Based on a complicated system of accounting, the general announced, FUNAI would be creating a special government fund made up of income gained from the sale of Indian products and the leasing of Indian lands. The money in this fund, according to the general, would go toward financing government-initiated agricultural and industrial projects on Indian reserves and would be coordinated with other schemes for regional development in Brazil. Eventually, the general argued, these programs would transform native hunting, fishing, and gardening economies and set the groundwork for the integration of Indians into the wider market economy and class structure of Brazil.[17]

The second measure of the new FUNAI regime was the announcement that Indian policy would be coordinated with the massive road-building program that was being planned for the Amazon region. In October 1970, for example, Brazilian President Médici announced that a contract was about to be signed between FUNAI and the Superintendency for the Development of the Amazon (SUDAM) for the pacification of nearly thirty Indian tribes who lived along the projected route of the new Trans-Amazon Highway. According to this contract, teams of FUNAI agents would be responsible for making contact with and pacifying hostile Indian tribes. Most important, FUNAI agents were expected to do two things: (1) insure that Indians did not serve as an obstacle to the rapid occupation of the Amazon Basin; and (2) provide highway workers with protection against a supposed Indian threat.[18]

At the time of the announcement of this contract, President Médici also made it known that a new Indian Statute was being formulated to provide directives for Indian policy in the Amazon Basin. The original draft of this Indian Statute was made public in October 1970 and contained several provisions that posed a threat to the continued territorial integrity of Indian tribes. One of the most extensive and clearly stated sections of the new Indian Statute, for example, empowered the president of Brazil, with the advice of FUNAI, to intervene in native areas and physically to relocate Indian tribes for six purposes:

1. to put an end to fighting between tribal groups;
2. to combat serious outbreaks of epidemics that may lead to the extermination of the native community or any disease that may endanger the integrity of the forest dweller or tribal group;
3. to maintain national security;
4. to carry out public works of interest to national development;
5. to repress widespread disorder or deforcement; and
6. to work valuable subsoil deposits of outstanding interest for national security and development.[19]

The significance of the above measures became clear in the spring of 1971. At that time, the Brazilian government revealed that a road connecting the small backwoods town of Xavantina with the settlement of Cachimbo in Mato Grosso (BR-080) was being planned to pass through a 40-kilometer section in the northern part of the Xingu National Park. Originally, government maps showed that this highway would pass outside of the limits of the Xingu National Park. The new plan called for a territorial invasion of the park.

The plan for the building of the BR-080 Highway shocked the Villas Boas brothers and produced a wave of protest throughout Brazil. A number of respected Brazilians voiced dissent with the new priorities of FUNAI and argued that the BR-080 Highway could easily be planned to bypass the Xingu National Park. This highway, these critics claimed, would bring an end to the successful Indianist experiment which the Villas Boas brothers had struggled to create over the past twenty years. "With the road," Orlando Villas Boas told the Brazilian press, "will come property seekers, and the Park will be definitively invaded and lost."[20]

High officials of FUNAI responded to these protests by claiming that the Xingu National Park was a "false experience" that was holding back the "progress and development" of Brazil. According to an official notice of FUNAI, the Xingu National Park was a "typical example of isolationism." The Xavantina–Cachimbo Highway, this notice declared, would be a "vital terrestrial link in the development and security of the country" and would "carry the Indians into a more intense participation" in the national economy.[21]

The president of FUNAI, General Oscar Jerônimo Bandeira de Mello, summed up the significance of the building of BR-080 Highway in the following words:

> The Indian is not a guinea pig, nor the property of a half a dozen opportunists. You cannot stop the development of Brazil on account of the Xingu Park.[22]

In late 1971, highway workers began construction activities on the Xavantina–Cachimbo Highway. One of the major groups affected by this highway was the Txukahamae tribe, a Gê-speaking people who inhabited the northernmost section of the Xingu National Park. For years, the Villas Boas brothers had been cultivating friendships with the Txukahamae chiefs, warning them about the dangerous diseases carried by settlers and trying to convince them to stay within the boundaries of the park. When the BR-080 Highway invaded the park, the Txukahamae split into two factions. One band, led by the chief Rauni, followed the Villas Boas brothers' advice and moved its village closer to the Diauarum Indian Post. A second band, led by a chief named Krumari, moved toward the highway workers and the road.

In November 1973, the *Jornal do Brasil* reported that a measles epidemic, carried by highway workers, had struck Krumari's band of the Txukahamae tribe. In the previous month, four Indians had died, and twenty more were in danger of losing their lives. Meanwhile, another seventy Txukahamae were moved to a government-run hospital at Santa Isabel do Morro in Araguaia, but doctors lacked the medicines to provide assistance to the tribe. "We are out of anti-biotics," a young doctor told the press, "and we urgently need vitamins, analgesics, and anti-fever drugs. The Indians are arriving with measles and broncho-pneumonia, and are in a critical state of malnutrition."[23]

A photograph that accompanied this report showed several Indians lying on mattresses on the hospital floor, covered only by sheets. To make matters even worse, in December 1973 another epidemic was reported to have struck the Txukahamae tribe. This time the carriers were said to be a group of farm workers who were clearing lands for cattle ranches along both sides of the Xavantina–Cachimbo Highway.[24]

The regime of Bandeira de Mello lasted from June 1970 to March 1974. During this period, a new model of Indian policy was institutionalized in Brazil. The main purposes of this model were: (1) to integrate Indians as rapidly as possible into the expanding market economy and class structure of Brazil; and (2) to insure that Indians did not serve as an obstacle to the occupation and settlement of the Amazon.

In the following chapters, I shall discuss what this new model of Indian policy has meant for the Indian tribes of the Amazon Basin. This discussion will begin with an assessment of the pacification program carried out by FUNAI along the Trans-Amazon

Highway network. I shall then turn to a discussion of FUNAI land policy and describe the effects that this policy has had on the Indian tribes in the Aripuanã Indian Park. Finally, I shall discuss the expanding mining frontier in the Amazon Basin and the nature of Indian policy presently being implemented along the Northern Perimeter and Manaus–Bôa Vista roads.

5

Pacification expeditions along the Trans-Amazon highway network

All through Brazilian history, from the most distant colonial times to the present day, the efforts for the "integration" of the Indian constituted the essential and almost sole object of official Indian policy. Throughout all the epochs, the "integration" of the Indian was promoted by just wars and forced pacification, by decimation, by forced labor, by religious conversion, and however many more techniques which were or continue to be imagined or suggested by interested sectors. . . . The Indian continues to be, today as always, the object of the same "integrationist" efforts.

> "The Indian and the Occupation of the Amazon," a document signed by eighty Brazilian ethnologists, anthropologists, sociologists, and historians, July 14, 1971

In October 1970, the Brazilian government began to construct a number of new pioneer highways across the Amazon Basin. Before this date, two major highways existed in the Amazon: the BR-010, or Belém–Brasília Highway, running north to south on the eastern edge of the Amazon; and the BR-364 Highway, connecting the city of Cuiabá in Mato Grosso with the town of Porto Velho in Rondônia. In 1970, the Brazilian government began constructing three other highways in the Amazon Basin: the 5,000-kilometer Trans-Amazon Highway, which ran east to west across the Amazon, from northeastern Brazil to the frontier with Peru; the BR-165, or Santarém–Cuiabá Highway, which ran north to south through west-central Brazil; and the BR-174 Highway, which connected the city of Manaus with the town of Bôa Vista (Roraima), along Brazil's northern frontier with Venezuela and Guyana. With the exception of the BR-174 Highway, all these roads were completed by 1974.

Several factors explain the rapidity with which Brazil was able to construct this highway network across the Amazon Basin. One of the most important factors was the role that the Brazilian National Highway Department (DNER) assumed in the planning of Brazil's massive highway construction program. The DNER was reorganized in 1969, and immediately began to draw up master plans for the integration of the entire federal highway network in Brazil. According to a document released by the Brazilian Ministry of Transportation, the main purpose of the DNER was "to form a unified network of highways in which both civil and military interests regarding national integration would be taken into account." By 1972, the DNER was one of the most modern state agencies of its kind in Latin America. Perhaps more than any other country in South America, Brazil was bureaucratically prepared to build a highway network across the Amazon Basin.[1]

Second, the Brazilian Army Corps of Engineers played a major role in the construction of the large Amazon highway network. From its inception, the Trans-Amazon highway program was a military effort in Brazil. Beginning in 1970, the Second Corps of army engineers started to build roads, lay railway tracks, set up communication lines, and construct sanitation facilities throughout the Amazon region. In the course of the highway construction program, it was responsible for consolidating overland communications between the Western Amazon region and the Center-West of Brazil, building a road across Acre to the Peruvian frontier, and constructing the Manaus–Bôa Vista and Santarém–Cuiabá highways. The large amount of technical expertise, heavy earthmoving equipment, and helicopter support available to these army engineers proved invaluable in the rapid construction of the Amazon roads.[2]

Third, over the past several years, the Brazilian government has been extremely successful in obtaining international loans to finance its federal highway construction program. Initially, this federal highway construction program was financed through a Special Road Fund from fuel and lubricant taxes, and with loans from the U.S. Agency for International Development (U.S. AID). In the late 1960s, however, the Brazilian government began to draw more heavily upon international loans for its highway construction program. Between 1968 and 1972, for example, the DNER received a total of $400 million in loans from the Inter-American Development and World banks. These loans represented the largest grants ever made to any country for highway construction in the history of the World Bank and were a major factor in the rapid growth of the Brazilian highway network.[3]

Fourth, foreign technical assistance was extremely important in the building of the Trans-Amazon highway network. One of the major areas of such technical assistance was in the provision of modern aerial-photographic and satellite-reconnaissance techniques. As far back as 1968, for example, U.S. AID provided an $8.4 million grant-in-aid to the Brazilian government for participation in the Earth Resources Observation Satellite Program (EROS) in the United States. Then, in 1970, the Brazilian government announced Project Radam (Radar Amazon), a huge aerial-photographic and mapping survey of the entire Amazon Basin.[4]

The major foreign company involved in Project Radam was the Aero Service Division of Litton Industries in the United States. In collaboration with the Goodyear Corporation and several Brazilian agencies and firms, Litton Industries carried out a detailed aerial mapping of the entire geology, hydrology, forestry, vegetation, and geography of the Amazon Basin. "Litton's work in Brazil for Project RADAM in association with LASA, the country's leading civil engineering firm," the president of the Aero Service Division was quoted as saying in 1972, "has accomplished in less than a year what would take conventional surveying expeditions a quarter century to complete."[5]

Finally, a number of multinational companies in Europe and the United States provided the Brazilian government with heavy earthmoving machinery for the building of the Amazon roads. One of the largest of these companies was the Brazilian subsidiary of the Caterpillar Tractor Company. Between 1970 and 1972, Caterpillar Brasil sold over 700 pieces of machinery worth $47 million to the Brazilian Army Corps of Engineers and to the seven private construction companies that were contracted to build the Trans-Amazon Highway. In 1972, Caterpillar alone controlled nearly 70 percent of the $125-million earthmoving market in Brazil. "Our market," a Caterpillar Brasil executive told a *Business Week* reporter, "will frequently grow faster than the GNP of a country, depending on how that country allocates its resources. This is particularly true in Brazil, where so much is being done in roads, airports, mining, and hydroelectric projects."[6]

All the above factors provide a context for understanding the critical situation Indian tribes faced along the margins of the Amazon roads. As mentioned in the previous chapter, in October 1970 the Brazilian National Indian Foundation (FUNAI) signed a contract with the Superintendency for the Development of the Amazon (SUDAM) for the pacification of Indian tribes along the Trans-Amazon and Santarém–Cuiabá highways. According to FUNAI, there were more than 5,000 Indians living in the area of these highways, dispersed in over twenty-nine different tribal groups. Twelve of these tribes had only had sporadic contacts with Brazilian society. Several others were hostile to foreign encroachments and had fought off outsiders in the past. Two of the earliest tribes to be pacified by FUNAI were the Parakanân and Kréen-Akaróre. It is instructive to consider what happened to these tribes as a result of FUNAI policy and the building of the roads.

The pacification of the Parakanân
and Kréen-Akaróre tribes

The Parakanân and their neighbors the Akuawa-Asuriní are a Tupi-speaking tribe located southwest of Belém in the State of Pará. The first contacts of the Parakanân with agents of Brazilian society occurred in the early 1950s when workers on the Tocantins Railroad began to clear a tract of forest through their lands. In 1953, the Brazilian Indian Protection Service (SPI) intervened in this area and made a first attempt to pacify the Parakanân tribe. At this time, the SPI established an Indian post in the area and placed 190 Indians under its protection. These first contacts proved devastating for the Parakanân tribe. Just a year following their initial pacification, over 50 Indians died from influenza and the remaining members of the Parakanân tribe escaped into the jungle and out of the reach of the SPI.[7]

Following this first experience, the Parakanân astutely avoided contacts with Brazilian settlers. Then, in 1970, the Brazilian government revealed that the new Trans-Amazon Highway would pass through the Territory of the Parakanân. In late 1970, FUNAI agents attempted to pacify and attract the Parakanân tribe. Again, this pacification expedition was disastrous for the tribe. Immediately following their pacification, forty members of the Parakanân tribe were stricken with influenza. Photographs taken a few weeks after this pacification expedition showed the Parakanân men with their bodies painted in black. Seemingly, the Parakanân had painted themselves black as a sign of mourning for the recently dead members of the tribe.[8]

By the spring of 1971, conditions grew progressively worse among the Parakanân tribe. At that time, workers along the Trans-Amazon Highway began to invade the territory of the tribe, although an Indian reserve had supposedly been decreed for the protection of the Parakanân. In the course of these initial contacts, highway workers were reported to have given presents to the Parakanân men and to have raped several Indian women.

Reports also noted that FUNAI agents had sexually violated some of the women of the tribe.[9]

In November 1971, a Brazilian physician named Antonio Madeiros visited a Parakanân village that was located 38 kilometers from the Trans-Amazon Highway. Madeiros reported that a "pattern of promiscuity" existed between outsiders and the Indians. In his medical investigations, Madeiros discovered that thirty-five Indian women and two FUNAI agents had venereal diseases. In addition, he found that eight children in the village had been born blind, and at least six others had recently died from dysentery. To make matters worse, in February 1972 another influenza epidemic struck the Parakanân tribe. This time a team of doctors was rushed to the Parakanân village, but without sufficient medicines or supplies they were of little use and several more Indians died.[10]

In May 1972, one of Brazil's most dedicated Indian agents, Antonio Cotrim Soares, resigned from FUNAI. Antonio Cotrim held an important position along the Trans-Amazon front, but had become disgusted with FUNAI's lack of support for him and other experienced Indian agents. The infection by venereal disease of the Parakanân tribe, Cotrim revealed in an interview with the Brazilian press, was not an isolated incident. It represented, he claimed, part of a brutal pattern that had come to characterize the situation of almost all the recently contacted tribes along the Trans-Amazon roads.[11]

In a highly publicized press interview, Cotrim described how he had been assigned to a pioneer front in the State of Pará and how a flu epidemic, brought by a visiting missionary, broke out among the Jandeavi tribe. According to Cotrim, he had sent an urgent message to the FUNAI headquarters asking for medical supplies, but it took more than forty-eight days for these supplies to arrive. By then, sixteen of the seventy-six members of the tribe had died.[12]

Most important, Cotrim's denunciations highlighted the economic directives that had increasingly come to characterize Indian policy in Brazil. "I am tired," Cotrim said at the time of his resignation from FUNAI in May 1972, "of being a grave-digger of the Indians. . . . I do not intend to contribute to enrichment of economic groups at the cost of the extinction of primitive cultures."[13]

According to Cotrim, Indian rights were being sacrificed for highway and development projects in Brazil. It was impossible, he argued, to protect these rights when the same agency, the Brazilian Ministry of the Interior, which had the responsibility for developing the interior, was also the controlling authority in Indian affairs.

A few months following Antonio Cotrim's resignation, a four-member team of the Aborigines Protection Society of London (APS) visited the Parakanân village, which was now called Espiritu Santo. The village was located just a few minutes' flying time from an airstrip built by a construction company along the Trans-Amazon Highway. In their report, the APS team wrote:

The hygiene was appalling, with excrement near the houses and one poor dog wandering around whose back was covered by a huge suppurating sore filled with flies and maggots. Eye disorders such as squints and (apparently) cataract [sic] were in evidence as were cysts and various growths, including a large tumor on a woman's head. Colds were also common and the risk of further infection from the nearby Trans-Amazonica was painfully apparent.[14]

According to the APS team, some of the Indians in this village were wearing clothes, but the majority were naked and without bodily ornaments. In fact, the APS team described the village itself as being barren of native artifacts, although some items gave the impression of a once-rich material culture. Since their pacification and resettlement, the APS team reported, these Indians had sold their cultural possessions to outsiders in exchange for guns and ammunition and were living off the dole of highway workers along the Trans-Amazon Highway. Most revealing, the population of the Parakanân had been reduced to eighty persons and there was every indication that their culture was rapidly being destroyed.[15]

Following the publication of the APS report, attention turned to the pacification of the Kréen-Akaróre tribe along the margins of the Santarém-Cuiabá Highway. The Kréen-Akaróre, mistakenly called "Brazil's Giant Indians," inhabited an area along the Peixoto de Azevado River in the Cachimbo forests of northern Mato Grosso. Adrian Cowell's famous documentary film, *The Tribe That Hides From Man*, brought these people to world attention through widespread television coverage in Europe and the United States. What has happened to these people since the making of Cowell's film is one of the most tragic stories in the modern history of Brazil.

As far back as 1950, the Villas Boas brothers had sighted eight Kréen-Akaróre villages from an airplane. Further, for many years, the brothers had news of their movements from the Kréen-Akaróre's traditional enemies, the Txukahamae tribe. During the 1950s, however, the Villas Boas brothers felt that there was no reason to make contact with the tribe, and hence for a period of years the Kréen-Akaróre were left alone in their tribal territory.

The first serious attempt to make contact with the tribe occurred in 1967 when a small band of Kréen-Akaróre was spotted at the Cachimbo Air Force Base. The presence of the Indians caused a wave of hysteria among the military personnel at the base, and a squadron of fighter planes combed the surrounding jungle in search of the tribe. At the time, Orlando Villas Boas was outraged by these actions and claimed that the military's fear of the Indians was totally unwarranted. The Kréen-Akaróre, he said, had come to the Cachimbo Air Force Base out of curiosity, as witnessed by the facts that they were accompanied by women and children and had left their bows, arrows, and baskets at one end of the base. Orlando Villas Boas was quoted as saying at this time:

Shout Indian and the whole world goes crazy. The *civilizados* shoot.
They fly airplanes all over the jungle. A brigadier is photographed
crouched behind a machine gun.[16]

Faced with such a delicate situation, in 1968 the Villas Boas
brothers were forced to carry out their first expedition to the
Kréen-Akaróre tribe. Initially, FUNAI gave the Villas Boas
brothers support for this expedition, but when it appeared that
peaceful contact would be difficult and take more time than originally thought, the Brazilian government cut off funds for the expedition. The result was that this first expedition failed. By 1970,
the Kréen-Akaróre had retreated deeper into the Cachimbo forest
and had burned their old villages and fields.

The inauguration of construction on the Santarém–Cuiabá
Highway in 1971 produced a final impetus for making contact
with the Kréen-Akaróre tribe. Again, FUNAI called upon Orlando and Claudio Villas Boas to direct this expedition.
Throughout 1971 and 1972, the Villas Boas brothers' approach
to the Kréen-Akaróre filled the pages of the Brazilian and the international press.

The Kréen-Akaróre were virtually being forced out of hiding in
order to make way for the Santarém–Cuiabá Highway. On one
side of the tribe was the Peixoto de Azevado River and the Xingu
National Park. On the other side was their traditional enemy, the
Apiaká tribe. Proceeding from the south and the east, sometimes
only days apart, were the forty-member Villas Boas brothers expedition team and topographic workers on the Santarém–Cuiabá
Highway.[17]

During the summer of 1972, one of the Kréen-Akaróre bands
closest to the new highway burned its village and attempted a
final retreat into the Cachimbo forest. This escape failed, however, and on February 5, 1973, thirty Indians, their heads shaven
and their bodies painted in black, entered the camp of Claudio
Villas Boas. One by one, each of the Kréen-Akaróre tribesmen
embraced the physically exhausted Indian agents, and then the
Indians and the agents exchanged gifts. The same day, Claudio

Villas Boas sent a radio message of the encounter with the Kréen-Akaróre to his absent brother Orlando, who was in São Paulo. Immediately, wire cables were monitored throughout the world. "Civilization," as one American newspaper put it, had finally "greeted" the elusive and hostile Kréen-Akaróre tribe.[18]

A few days following the February 1973 encounter, Orlando Villas Boas went before the Brazilian press. With a sense of seriousness and urgency, he explained in minute detail the history of his experience with the Kréen-Akaróre tribe: the first sighting of eight villages in 1950; the unsuccessful expeditions in 1967 and 1968; the hardships, frustrations, and purposes of the recent expedition; the present fears and promises made to the Indians. At the start of the most recent Kréen-Akaróre expedition, Orlando Villas Boas noted that he had told the press that a "crime" was about to be committed and that his and Claudio's efforts were merely meant to lessen the degree of violence implicit in that "crime." The Kréen-Akaróre, he said,

lived in happiness until the day that an airplane spotted them. That day began another tragedy for an Indian nation. It consoles us some, and we are concentrating all out efforts in this, that the crime would be greater if there was no such mediating force, trying to avoid the inevitable clash between two civilizations.[19]

Finally, Orlando Villas turned to the reporters present and his self-consciously chosen words became poignant in tone. "If a Reserve," he said, "is not immediately demarcated for the Kréen-Akaróre, and if a positive policy of protection is not developed in collaboration with those responsible for the construction of the Santarém–Cuiabá Highway, then the Kréen-Akaróre, like so many other Indian nations, will inexorably disappear. It will mean their final destruction."[20]

A month following this interview, Brazilian President Médici signed a decree for the creation of a Kréen-Akaróre reserve. Against the advice of the Villas Boas brothers, however, this decree did not include in the reserve the traditional territory of the Kréen-Akaróre tribe. Further, it made the Santarém–Cuiabá

Highway one of the boundaries of the reserve. Within months, this action proved devastating for the remaining 300 members of the Kréen-Akaróre tribe.[21]

In January 1974, less than a year after the pacification of the Kréen-Akaróre, Brazilian newspapers cited a firsthand report on what was happening to the tribe. This report was written by Ezequias Paulo Heringer, an Indian agent commissioned to investigate conditions along the Kréen-Akaróre front. According to Heringer, the Kréen-Akaróre were dispersed along the Santarém–Cuiabá Highway, fraternizing with truck drivers, and begging for food.

In his report, Heringer charged that an Indian agent named Antonio Souza Campinas had forcibly relocated the Kréen-Akaróre to the margins of the Santarém–Cuiabá Highway. Apparently, several Indian agents, including Orlando and Claudio Villas Boas, had warned high officials of FUNAI against the placement of Campinas as the director of the Kréen-Akaróre Reserve. According to these agents, Campinas was known to be irresponsible and to have committed serious sexual crimes against Indians in other areas of Brazil.

Heringer told the Brazilian press that the Kréen-Akaróre had abandoned their gardens and were in a state of sickness, hunger, and despair. In one account, he was quoted as saying:

We found two temporary houses along the Santarém–Cuiabá Highway and a population of 35 persons, all suffering from colds, including the Kréen-Akaróre chief, Iaquil, who did not know where he was. . . . The customs of the tribe have degenerated, and tobacco and alcohol now form part of their new habits.[22]

Within a year, the population of the Kréen-Akaróre tribe had been reduced from approximately 300 to less than 135. Then, in 1974, Orlando and Claudio Villas Boas began a campaign for the removal of the Kréen-Akaróre to the Xingu National Park. From the beginning of their efforts to make contact with the Kréen-Akaróre, the Villas Boas brothers had been against such removal.

They had hoped that the Brazilian government would demarcate a reserve for the tribe and protect the Indians from highway workers and other elements along the Santarém–Cuiabá road. When this proved not to be the case, the Villas Boas brothers were forced to intervene and relocate the Kréen-Akaróre as they had previously done in the late 1960s and early 1970s with the devastated Txikão and Beiço-de-Pau tribes.[23]

In October 1974, the Villas Boas brothers commissioned an airplane to transfer the Kréen-Akaróre to the Xingu National Park. At the time of this transfer, it became known that another epidemic was ravishing the remaining 135 members of the tribe. A Brazilian doctor aboard this airplane reported that the Kréen-Akaróre women were purposely aborting their children, rather than produce offspring who would face the new conditions of the tribe. Since this date, the Kréen-Akaróre have been living next to their traditional enemies, the Txukahamae tribe, in the northern part of the Xingu National Park.[24]

Indian policy and the Trans-Amazon highway system: an overview

The decimations of the Parakanân and Kréen-Akaróre tribes described in this chapter were not isolated incidents, but formed part of a more global pattern of ethnic destruction that since 1970 has encompassed the entire Amazon region of Brazil. Between 1970 and 1974, the Brazilian government tried to speed up the processes of "national integration" by building a series of highways through Indian parks and reserves. The traumatic and disastrous effects of this "integration" program on Indian tribes have been documented in International Red Cross, Survival International, and Aborigines Protection Society (APS) reports on Indian policy in Brazil.

More recently, Edwin Brooks, a geographer and one of the original members of the APS team, has published a number of articles on the scope and consequences of highway invasions in indigenous areas of the Amazon Basin. One of these articles was titled, "The Brazilian Road to Ethnicide." This article contained a series of federal, state, and territorial maps that showed highways were being planned to pass through almost every major Indian park and reserve in the Amazon of Brazil (see Map 3). Repeating the conclusions of the earlier APS report, Brooks wrote that "once development interests are involved, Indian Reserves are hardly worth the maps they are drawn on."[25]

For many journalists and popular writers, the uprooting of Indian tribes caused by these highways was seen as one of the tragic, but inevitable, costs of "economic progress" in Brazil. According to these writers, the destruction of the aboriginal populations of the Amazon Basin was a sad, but necessary, consequence of an extremely advanced technological society experiencing rapid economic growth.

Unfortunately, this position, which contains only a modicum of truth, has tended to obscure any genuine public understanding of the nature of Indian policy in Brazil. The example of the Xingu National Park provides a concrete case where, at least until relatively recently, more than a dozen Indian tribes have been protected against the dangers of frontier expansion, and where Indians have been provided with the medical conditions and land base to survive. The Amazon Basin is such a vast geographical area that other Indian parks and reserves could have been created *on the model* of the Xingu National Park. The Brazilian government, in other words, could have intervened to protect these Indian land areas against outside encroachments, and could have planned highway and development projects so as not to have threatened the territorial integrity of Indian tribes.[26]

For a brief period in 1968, this appeared as if it might be the policy of FUNAI. By 1970, however, new directives of an in-

Map 3. Indians and the Trans-Amazon highway system
Source: E. Brooks, "Frontiers of Ethnic Conflict in the Brazilian Amazon," *International Journal of Environmental Studies*, 7 (1974), 68.

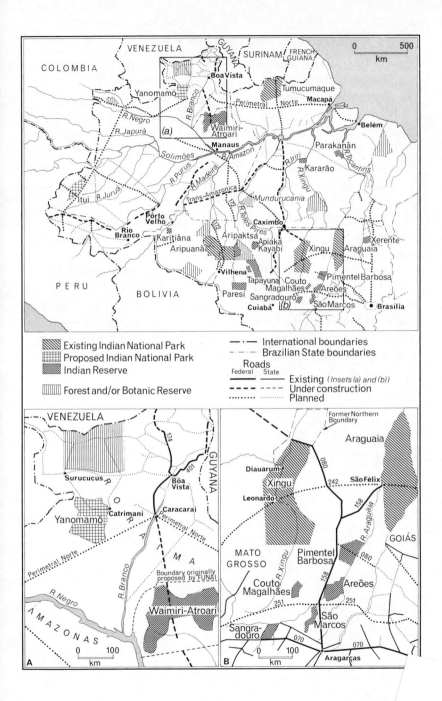

Existing Indian National Park
Proposed Indian National Park
Indian Reserve

Forest and/or Botanic Reserve

International boundaries
Brazilian State boundaries

Roads
Federal State

Existing (Insets (a) and (b))
Under construction
Planned

tegrationist and developmental nature began to dominate Brazilian Indian policy, and a number of Indian tribes, such as the Parakanân and Kréen-Akaróre, were uprooted and destroyed.

Between 1970 and 1974, Brazilian Indian policy became increasingly compromised with the larger economic development policies of the Brazilian military regime. During this period, the Brazilian National Indian Foundation became a chief accomplice in the processes of ethnocide that were unleashed on the Indian tribes of the Amazon Basis. Its "reformed" Indian policy, to state the situation most simply, tended to speed up, rather than stop, the processes of ethnic destruction that have so bitterly characterized the frontier history of Brazil.

Obviously, it is necessary to make a deeper analysis of the motives behind Indian and development policies in the Amazon region of Brazil. Why, one may ask, did the Brazilian government choose to build these roads at such great human, social, and cultural costs? Or more concretely, for whom were these new highways actually being built, and why was it necessary to construct them through Indian parks and reserves?

6

The invasion
of the Aripuanã Indian Park

The area of the Aripuanã Indian Park has one of the richest deposits of tin in the world, and there are big national and international mining companies anxious to get in there. They are not prepared to wait five, ten, or twenty years while the Indians are contacted, pacified, and prepared for integration into our society. Brazil is trying to speed up the process of contacting the Indians, but we do not know where to go.

> Eduardo Galvão, Brazilian anthropologist, quoted in "Progress, Indians Collide in Brazil," *Los Angeles Times*, April 26, 1973

In their report for the Aborigines Protection Society of London (APS), Edwin Brooks, René Fuerst, John Hemming, and Francis Huxley described the severe threat to Indians that resulted from the absence of a coherent land policy on the part of FUNAI. The APS report noted that the reserve system of FUNAI tended to diminish Indian land areas and posed a threat to the biological and cultural integrity of Indian tribes. By legal right, the APS report stated, Indian parks and reserves belonged to the Brazilian government as part of the so-called Indian Estate and could be sold or leased by FUNAI. Further, many tribes did not even live in well-defined Indian parks and reserves and were being uprooted by agricultural and mining companies interested in gaining possession of Indian lands. "Unless the law safeguarding their homelands is enforced," the APS team wrote in 1973, "the Indians will be swept away by the advancing frontier of colonisation and economic exploitation."[1]

Previous to the building of the Trans-Amazon Highway, the

major economic agents who posed a threat to the territorial integrity of Indian tribes were small-scale rubber collectors, nut gatherers, diamond prospectors, and backwoods farmers, hunters, and traders. The new highway and development program in the Amazon introduced two additional economic elements along Brazil's northern and western frontiers. The first of these new elements was the Brazilian government itself, which, as we have previously seen, initiated a massive program of highway construction, mineral exploration, and agricultural colonization in the Amazon region. The second element was a number of powerful private, state, and multinational corporations that wanted to gain access to the rich agricultural, mineral, and timber resources of the region. The presence of both these elements reflected a broader economic transformation that was taking place throughout Brazil. In the wake of this transformation, several important changes took place in the land and resource policies of FUNAI.

One of the major areas where FUNAI accommodated its land policy to the interests of these new economic elements was in the vast jungle region along the Aripuanã and Roosevelt rivers. According to ethnological accounts, at one time there were more than 10,000 native people in this area living in more than 100 village encampments. The largest of these tribes were the Suruí and the Cintas Largas, the latter of which was named after the wide bark-cloth belts worn by the men of the tribe. Other tribes in this area, most of whom spoke Tupi-Kawahib languages, were the Bôcas-Negras, Rama-Rama, Itogapúk, Pahim, Aipo-Sessí, Pawaté, Majubim, Mialat, Paranawát, Wiraféd, Takuatep, and Ipotewat.[2]

For nearly a century, the Indian tribes of this region had successfully fought off rubber collectors and diamond prospectors who periodically attempted to invade their lands. Then, in the early 1960s, a number of large Brazilian real estate companies began to take an interest in the lands of the Aripuanã region. One of these companies was the Brazilian rubber-extraction firm of

Arruda and Junqueira, which maintained a number of outposts in the Brazilian Territory of Rondônia.

In 1963, a man named Francisco de Brito, who worked for the Arruda and Junqueira firm, organized a band of prospectors (*garimpeiros*) and gunslingers (*pistoleiros*) to clear the Cintas Largas off their lands. According to accounts of this incident, which later became known as the "Massacre at Parallel Eleven," de Brito hired a plane to attack one of the Cintas Largas villages from the air. At the time of this attack, the Cintas Largas were performing an important tribal ceremony. Supposedly, at mid-day, the airplane carrying de Brito and his henchmen arrived at the Cintas Largas village and packets of sugar were dropped on the Indians below. Then, the plane swept down and proceeded to dynamite the Indian village. No one knows exactly how many Indians were killed in this attack. Some of the Indians, however, did escape, and another expedition was organized to wipe out the tribe.

The gory details of both of these attempts to exterminate the Cintas Largas tribe, as well as the unsuccessful and short-lived government investigation of the massacre, were described in Norman Lewis's article, "Genocide – From Fire and Sword to Arsenic and Bullets, Civilization Has Sent Six Million Indians to Extinction." One of the most overlooked aspects of Lewis's description of the "Massacre at Parallel Eleven" was his suggestion that valuable mineral deposits might have been a primary reason for the organized attempt to destroy the tribe. The tragedy of the Cintas Largas, Lewis wrote,

was that deposits of rare metals were being found in the area. What these metals were, it was not clear. Some sort of security blackout has been imposed, only fitfully penetrated by vague news reports of the activities of American and European companies, and of the smuggling of plane-loads of the said rare metals back to the USA.[3]

Lewis based this suggestion on the recorded testimony of two witnesses in the Cintas Largas case. One of these witnesses was a man named Ataide Pereira, who formed part of the second de Brito expedition against the Cintas Largas and who related the details of this expedition to a Jesuit priest named Father Edgar Smith. Lewis quoted Pereira's account of this expedition as follows:

It took us six weeks to find the Cintas Largas and about a week to get back. . . . Chico [the nickname for de Brito] found some minerals and took them back to keep the company pleased. The fact is the Indians are sitting on valuable land and doing nothing with it. They've got a way of finding the best plantation land and there's all these valuable minerals about too. They have to be persuaded to go, and if all else fails, well then, it has to be force.[4]

The second witness Lewis cited was a priest named Father Valdemar Veber. Seemingly, in 1964, Father Veber gave testimony before a police inspector in Cuiabá, Mato Grosso, who was carrying out an official investigation of the Cintas Largas case. In his testimony, Father Veber was quoted by Lewis as saying:

It is not the first time that the firm of Arruda and Junqueira has committed crimes against Indians. A number of expeditions have been organized in the past. This firm acts as a cover for other undertakings who are interested in acquiring land or who plan to exploit the rich mineral deposits existing in this area.[5]

Throughout the late 1960s, evidence began to accumulate that large deposits of cassiterite, a key material in the production of tin, had been discovered in the Brazilian Territory of Rondônia. In 1967, for example, the *Christian Science Monitor* carried an article titled, "Brazil Becoming Self-Sufficient in Tin." This article described how over the previous decade a vast new mining frontier had been opened up in the Territory of Rondônia. According to this article, a handful of large international companies had installed modern mechanized-mining operations in Rondônia and were slowly making Brazil self-sufficient in tin.[6]

One of the largest of these companies was Mineraçâo Ferro-Union (FERUSA), a multinational subsidiary of Billiton International Metals, a unit of Royal Dutch Shell. By 1967, FERUSA had invested more than $3 million in its Rondônia tin deposits and had discovered over 4,000 metric tons of tin. According to a Dutch geologist who worked for FERUSA, the company was interested in a 720,000-acre concession in Rondônia and was presently carrying out several projects in exploration and prospecting. Twelve other large companies, besides FERUSA, were also exploring in Rondônia and three companies were operating mines.[7]

In 1968, a major boost was giving to this mining frontier when the Brazilian Army Corps of Engineers completed a 900-mile road between Cuiabá and Porto Velho, the capital of the Territory of Rondônia. Major financial and technical assistance for this road-building project came from the U.S. Army, which contributed $1 million worth of heavy construction equipment to the Brazilian Army Corps of Engineers, and from the U.S. Agency for International Development (U.S. AID), which lent Brazil $2.6 million, as part of the Alliance for Progress, for the construction of fourteen permanent bridges along the road. By the late 1960s, fifty heavy vehicles were reported to enter and leave the town of Porto Velho each day. Most of these vehicles were trucks carrying cassiterite to tin factories and smelters in the South of Brazil.[8]

From the beginning of the tin-mining boom in Rondônia a series of problems arose between the new mining companies and individual prospectors who had formerly dominated the economy of the region. Until the late 1960s, the Territory of Rondônia was a typical frontier area in Brazil, relatively free from police and government control, and plagued by crime, prostitution, and real estate swindles. Then, in April 1970, the National Department of Mineral Production (DNPM), a coordinating agency for mineral licensing in Brazil, passed a decree that outlawed all individual prospecting in Rondônia. As a result of this decree, by March 1971 almost all mining activities in Rondônia were in the hands of large domestic and international firms. Fifteen-hundred prospectors in Rondônia were given jobs by these new companies, and another 2,000 prospectors were asked by the federal government to leave the territory.

At the same time, several new companies began to enter the region. One of these companies was Cia. Estanífera do Brasil (CESBRA), a newly organized Brazilian tin-mining company jointly owned by Compagnie Française d'Enterprises Minières Métallurgiques et d'Investissements (COFREMMI), a French affiliate of the Patiño Tin Syndicate, and by Antonio Sanchez Galdeano, a rich Brazilian industrialist. Other international companies that made smaller investments in Rondônia during this period were the Molybdenum Corporation of America, the Grace Ore and Mining Company, and NL Industries, all of the United States.[9]

By the early 1970s, in other words, several important changes had taken place in the economic structure of Rondônia. These changes formed part of a more global transformation in the Brazilian mining sector and reflected the new symbiosis that, on the national level, had emerged between the military government and a number of large multinational corporations. The effects of these changes were immediately felt by the remaining members of the Cintas Largas and Suruí tribes.

The disintegration
of the Cintas Largas and Suruí tribes

Following the publicity surrounding the "Massacre at Parallel Eleven," the Brazilian government promised that it would intervene in the Territory of Rondônia to provide protection for Indian tribes. In 1967, for example, two of Brazil's most respected Indian agents, Francisco and Apoena Meirelles, made contact with several Cintas Largas bands and convinced their chiefs to remain at or near a newly constructed Indian post. At the same time, the government announced the creation of the Aripuanã

Indian Park, a special area to be set aside for the protection of the Cintas Largas and Suruí tribes.[10]

The decree establishing the Aripuanã Indian Park was important for two reasons. First, it indicated the intention of the government to intervene in this area and to set aside a specific reserve for the protection of the Cintas Largas and Suruí. Second, it also stated that such protection *did not* imply the abandonment of the rich mineral resources contained on Indian lands.

In an official letter to the president of Brazil following the creation of the Aripuanã Indian Park, the Brazilian minister of the interior, José Costa Cavalcanti, stated that these mineral deposits were of "great importance" to national development, but were presently threatened by unlicensed prospectors who were carrying out exploration activities within the limits of the park. Under the direction of FUNAI, the minister's letter claimed, Indian property rights would be respected, but without the abandonment of these important sources of mineral wealth.[11]

For a period of time, very little attention focused upon these mineral provisions and it appeared as if the government was serious about providing protection to the Cintas Largas and Suruí. Then, in December 1971, the Brazilian press carried a series of stories about a supposed "Indian uprising" in the Aripuanã National Park. When this incident was first reported, very little was known beyond the facts that a former journalist, at the time in the employ of FUNAI, and a radio telegrapher had been killed. Nevertheless, rumors quickly spread about a war between Indians and government agents along this section of the national frontier.

A few days after this incident, the president of FUNAI, General Oscar Jerônimo Bandeira de Mello, placed the blame for these killings on certain "hostile" members of the Cintas Largas tribe. According to the general, Indian agents had made several attempts to approach and pacify the Cintas Largas, but the Indians had refused their gifts and assumed a belligerent stance against the presence of government agents on their lands. In a special press interview on the Cintas Largas attack, Minister of the Interior Costa Cavalcanti made a similar claim. The Indians, he said, were by nature a "nomadic people" and the incident resulted from their "geographic ignorance" of the region. A special military unit, the minister revealed, had been dispatched to maintain order and to protect settlers in the area surrounding the Aripuanã Indian Park.[12]

In the months between December 1971 and the spring of 1972, an entirely different story of this incident emerged in the pages of the Brazilian press. Seemingly, since the creation of the Aripuanã Indian Park in 1968, FUNAI and other agencies within the Ministry of the Interior had authorized mineral prospecting and colonization companies to enter the park. One large company, the Itaporanga firm, owned by the Melhorança family of São Paulo, was reported to have settled over 500 families in the area of the park. In addition, a mineral exploration company had been granted a license to prospect in the area. For months previous to the supposed "Indian uprising," according to reports in the Brazilian press, the Cintas Largas chiefs had communicated their discontent with these land encroachments to Indian agents, and several messages had been sent to the FUNAI central offices in Brasília pleading for the protection of the park.[13]

In March 1972, Apoena Meirelles, the director of the Aripuanã Indian Park, sent a formal letter to FUNAI describing how settlers had invaded the park, causing bloody clashes with Indians and carrying fatal diseases. Meirelles told the Brazilian press that FUNAI had done nothing to remove these settlers from the park, nor would it give him permission to do so as its director. Meirelles expressed his views on the situation in the Aripuanã Indian Park in the following words:

In less than four years, the lands of the Cintas Largas and the Suruí have been divested. Epidemics have already left their mark, and the tribes have already begun the first steps down the long road to misery, hunger, and the prostitution of their women. . . . I would rather die fighting alongside the Indians in defense of their lands and their rights to live than see them tomorrow reduced to beggars on their own lands.[14]

Revelations of these sorts continued to appear throughout 1972 and 1973. In August 1972, for example, the Aborigines Protection Society (APS) team attempted to gain permission to visit the Aripuanã Indian Park. Although they were refused permission, the APS team found that the original limits of the park had been severely reduced, that its former southern boundary had been occupied by a new highway, and that a São Paulo development company had brought settlers into the region. In their report, the APS team wrote:

The ceding of this huge slice of excellent land appeared to be the most recent example of surrender of Indian land to outside colonizers. We discovered it only by comparing various maps. It appeared to be as bad as the worst example of the practice that reached scandalous proportions in the last days of the SPI.[15]

A few months later, in November 1972, another report appeared that corroborated the situation described by Meirelles and the APS team. This report was written by Jean Chiappino, a French physician who had spent several months among the Cintas Largas and Suruí tribes. In an urgent message sent to the Eighth Regional Delegation of FUNAI in Porto Velho and published in the Brazilian press, Chiappino stated that the Suruí Indians located at the Sete de Setembro Indian Post were in an extremely critical state and had been practically decimated by tuberculosis. Since July 1972, his message noted, twenty Indians had died, and several more, including Dikboba, the chief of the band, were now in a grave state of health. Over 40 percent of the tribe was suffering from pulmonary infections, and many of the Indians had run off into the jungle to escape the oppressive conditions at the Indian post. Chiappino stressed the need for immediate medical action by FUNAI and petitioned that assistance be sought from the International Red Cross.

Even more serious, Chiappino noted in his message of November 1972 that seven large companies were carrying out mineral exploration activities in the Aripuanã Indian Park and that these companies posed a critical social and medical threat to the more numerous Cintas Largas tribe. The seven companies mentioned by Chiappino were Mineração São Marcos Ltd., Cia. Espírito Santo de Mineração (CESMI), Sociedade de Mineração Atlântico (SOMINA), Mineração Vale de Madeira Limited (MIVALE), Mineração Vale do Roosevelt, Cia Estanífera do Brasil (CESBRA), and Mineração Alcione.[16]

All these companies were attempting to cash in on the new cassiterite boom in Rondônia and had been given authorization to prospect in the Aripuanã Indian Park by FUNAI. Five of the companies were linked to Cia. Estanífera do Brasil (CESBRA) and formed part of the Patiño tin-mining group.[17]

Recently, Chiappino has published a more detailed report, under the auspices of the International Work Group for Indigenous Affairs in Copenhagen and Amazind in Geneva, which describes conditions in the Aripuanã Indian Park since the filing in November 1972 of his urgent message calling for International Red Cross assistance. In this report, Chiappino points out that despite his medical warnings to FUNAI, the tuberculosis epidemic that he initially witnessed had struck all age groups in the Suruí band, bringing death to the Indians within the short space of two months. The initial symptom of this disease was a hoarse cough which filled the forest at night. This was followed by an "expectoration . . . which exhausted the patient," and "a permanent fever." The development of this syndrome was quicker among Indian children, and "carried off its victims in terminal cachexia." The spread of this epidemic, Chiappino claims, "distressed, disoriented, and destroyed" Indian families and the social group. According to his calculations, over 60 percent of the Suruí population observed was affected by this epidemic alone.

In his report, Chiappino also describes how he attempted to control this epidemic by providing an antituberculosis treatment, but how he was hampered by the small and incompetent medical staff of FUNAI. The presence of certain cases of hepatitis among the Suruí, he claims, was caused by FUNAI medical personnel who did not take even the most minimal precautions in giving injections to the Indians.[18]

Most significant, at the time of his departure from Brazil, Chiappino claims, there was no indication that FUNAI had created a policy for the effective protection of native resources and lands. To the contrary, settlers and mineral companies were continuing to invade the Aripuanã Indian Park. Numerous landing strips had been constructed in the area. Game was beginning to become critically scarce. According to Chiappino, the existence of these conditions was a logical result of the land and leasing policies of FUNAI.[19]

In essence, the Cintas Largas and Suruí were merely the first indigenous groups to feel the effects of the new mineral boom that was taking place throughout the Amazon Basin of Brazil. In February 1972, for example, the *Engineering and Mining Journal*, a glossy monthly publication of the international mining industry, carried an article titled, "The Amazon Basin – New Mineral Province for the 70s." According to this article, over fifty international corporations were already involved in mining development projects in the Amazon Basin, lured on by Brazilian tax incentives, political stability, and government exploration aids. Among the companies in the Brazilian Amazon by this date were Bethlehem Steel Corporation, U.S. Steel Corporation, the Aluminum Company of Canada, Kaiser Aluminum Company, Reynolds Metals, Rio Tinto Zinc Corporation, Union Carbide Corporation, International Nickel Company, W. R. Grace and Company, and Companhia Vale do Rio Doce (CVRD), the large state-owned mining company in Brazil. The *Engineering and Mining Journal* article stated:

Brazil's forbidding Amazon Basin, virtually impenetrable and untouched by modern technology, is now moving into the spotlight as one of the most promising undeveloped mineral provinces in the world.

. . . Although most big new mining ventures will probably end up with Brazilian state or private control, foreign companies generally are eager for any piece of the action they can get.[20]

The new mining boom in the Amazon provides a basis for understanding recent Indian policies in Brazil. When the Trans-Amazon highway program was begun in 1970, the role of the Brazilian National Indian Foundation was mainly to pacify Indian tribes. More recently, with these highways built or near completion, FUNAI has been called upon, often against the wishes of its leadership and various dedicated Indian agents, to make way for multinational and state-owned companies who are interested in gaining access to the natural resources of the Amazon Basin. Basically, the response of FUNAI to this new challenge has been a simple one. In recent years, FUNAI has institutionalized a policy, similar to that practiced by the Bureau of Indian Affairs in the United States, of leasing the rich mineral resources contained on Indian lands. As will be shown in the next chapter, at present these leasing policies provide one of the greatest threats to the continuing territorial integrity and survival of Brazilian Indian tribes.

7

Indian policy and the Amazon mining frontier

My task will be to integrate the Indian into national society, because it is impossible to stop the process of development of the country with the argument that Indians should be protected and maintained in their pure state.

General Ismarth de Araújo Oliveira, president of the Brazilian National Indian Foundation (FUNAI)

This is a promise that I can strongly make: we are going to create a policy of integrating the Indian population into Brazilian society as rapidly as possible. . . . We think that the ideals of preserving the Indian population within its own "habitat" are very beautiful ideas, but unrealistic.

Mauricio Rangel Reis, Brazilian minister of the interior, March 1974

In May 1973, a short article by a U.S. Geological Survey geologist named Max White, "Probing the Unknown Amazon Basin – A Roundup of 21 Mineral Exploration Programs in Brazil," appeared in the *Engineering and Mining Journal*. White's article described twenty-one geological and mineral projects being undertaken in the Amazon Basin as part of a cooperative program between the Brazilian Department of Mineral Production, the Mineral Resources Research Company, and the U.S. Geological Survey, under the sponsorship of the Brazilian government and the U.S. Agency for International Development (U.S. AID). According to White, by this date, there were 225 geologists and engineers conducting mineral investigations in the Amazon – more than 125 at Belém, about 40 at Manaus, and about 60 at Porto Velho.

89

One of the major areas of mineral exploration at this time was in the northwestern part of the Amazon Basin in the Brazilian Territory of Roraima and the State of Amazonas. White's article described at least three major projects in this region: (1) the North Amazonia project, which consisted of a 1,051,840-square-kilometer geological and geochemical reconnaissance of most of the territory of Brazil north of the Amazon River; (2) the Roraima project, which consisted of geologic work in a 120,000-square-kilometer area in the northernmost part of the Territory of Roraima, near the border with Guyana and Venezuela; and (3) the Aripuanã-Sucunduri project, which covered an 80,000-square-kilometer area in the drainage systems of the Aripuanã, Roosevelt, Guariba, Juma, and Sucunduri rivers, in the southeastern part of the State of Amazonas.[1]

At least three factors explain the large amount of mineral-exploration activities that have taken place in the northwestern part of the Amazon Basin in recent years. The first, and perhaps most important, factor was the completion of Project Radam, the huge aerial-photographic and mineral reconnaissance survey of the Amazon Basin. By 1973, when White published his article, geologists from Project Radam had nearly completed an examination of the entire northern section of the Amazon. According to mining journal reports, large deposits of iron ore, manganese, tin, bauxite, and coal had been found in this region. In the Territory of Roraima, a number of radioactive anomalies had been noted, indicating significant deposits of uranium. Elsewhere, in the northern region, Project Radam had discovered large deposits of columbium, tantalum, zirconium, gold, and diamonds. The results of these aerial-photographic surveys indicated that the Amazon Basin contained one of the most valuable and diverse mineral profiles in the world.[2]

Second, from 1970 onward, the state-owned Companhia Vale do Rio Doce (CVRD) expressed its willingness to join with foreign companies in order to finance large-scale mining projects in the Amazon Basin. The first of these projects, which would

cost an estimated $3 billion (American billion) when completed
in 1980, was the early joint venture between the U.S. Steel Corporation and CVRD for the mining of iron ore in the Serra dos
Carajas. Another joint venture was Mineração Rio do Norte, a
company that was formed in order to mine the large bauxite deposits discovered along the Trombetas River in northern Pará.[3]

Mineração Rio do Norte was created in 1973 after a period of
intense bauxite exploration by several international companies
and following the nationalization of foreign-owned bauxite
mines in neighboring Guyana. When completed in 1977, Mineração Rio do Norte was expected to be one of the largest mining
projects of its kind in the world. Included in the original agreement to form the company were: Companhia Vale do Rio Doce
(41 percent), Alcan Aluminum Company of Canada (19 percent), Cia. Brasileira de Aluminio (10 percent), Aardal of Sunn-
dal Verk of Sweden, Norsk Hydro of Norway, the National Institute of Industry of Spain, Reynolds Aluminum Company of the
United States, Rio Tinto Zinc of Britain, and Mineração Rio
Xingu of Brazil (all owning 5 percent).[4]

Finally, throughout this period, the new state-owned Mineral
Resources Research Company (CPRM) played an extremely important role in opening up the Amazon mining frontier. CPRM
was created by the government in 1969 and has since served three
important functions in Brazil: (1) to improve the basic geological
knowledge of the country; (2) to provide financial and technical
assistance to other companies, both foreign and domestic, for exploration and mine development; and (3) to sponsor and develop
the technological base for a rapidly expanding mineral industry
in Brazil.

Between July 1970 and March 1975, CPRM mapped over 2
million square kilometers of Brazilian territory and financed over
thirty-three mineral exploration projects. One of CPRM's major
projects, which was completed in 1975, was the exploration of
large molybdenum deposits in the Serra do Mel region, north of
Bôa Vista near the Venezuelan frontier. Other major projects

were lignite, peat, and saprolite explorations along the Jutaí River in the State of Amazonas, and an evaluation of large titanium reserves along the Uaupés and Tapuruquara rivers in the far western part of the Brazilian Amazon. Map 4 shows the several mineral exploration projects being carried out or financed by CPRM as of 1975, along with the approximate location of various Indian parks and other major mining projects in the Amazon Basin of Brazil.[5]

To gain access to these newly discovered mineral reserves, in 1973 the Brazilian government began construction on two major highways in the northern and western parts of the Amazon Basin. The first of these was the 2,500-mile Northern Perimeter Road. When completed, this highway would traverse the entire northern part of the Amazon, skirting the borders between Brazil and the neighboring countries of Surinam, Guyana, Venezuela, Colombia, and Peru. The second highway, which formed part of the Trans-Amazon network and which cut across the Northern Perimeter in a north-south direction, was the BR-174 or Manaus–Bôa Vista Road (see Map 3, Inset a).[6]

In 1973, the Brazilian National Indian Foundation (FUNAI) also announced its intention to carry out pacification expeditions in the northwestern part of the Amazon Basin. At the time of this announcement, high officials of FUNAI claimed that it would be one of the most difficult tasks in the history of the agency. One report estimated that there were between 20,000 and 50,000 Indians in this area living in over 270 tribal or subtribal groups. Two of the largest tribes in this area are the Waimirí-Atroarí along the Manaus–Bôa Vista Highway and the Yanomamö in the Territory of Roraima. A discussion of the present situation of these two tribes provides further insight into the ways that FUNAI has sacrificed Indian land rights in order to make way for highway and mining development projects in Brazil.[7]

The pacification of the Waimirí-Atroarí tribe

The Waimirí-Atroarí number more than 2,000 people and live in a large jungle refuge area between the Alalau, Uatuma, and Jauaperi rivers north of Manaus. For more than a century, the Waimirí-Atroarí had successfully defended their territory against all outside encroachments and attacks. Then, in the late 1960s, several new attempts were made to contact the tribe. In 1968, for example, an Italian Catholic priest named Father Giovanni Caleri attempted to pacify the Waimirí-Atroarí tribe. This attempt, however, failed, and the Waimirí-Atroarí gained notoriety by killing Father Caleri and eight other members of his pacification team.[8]

In the early 1970s, the Brazilian government decreed a special reserve for the Waimirí-Atroarí in the State of Amazonas. At the same time, however, it also began to lay plans for a road that would connect the city of Manaus with Bôa Vista and pass through the new Waimirí-Atroarí Indian Reserve. This road was of strategic military and economic significance in Brazil. It provided the only military route to the Venezuelan frontier and terminated, in the north, at the large molybdenum deposits discovered by CPRM geologists in the Serra do Mel (see Project 12, Map 4).

In 1974, with highway construction taking place throughout the entire northwestern part of the Brazilian Amazon, scores of FUNAI agents were sent to the Waimirí-Atroarí front. Almost weekly, helicopters flew over Waimirí-Atroarí villages dropping gifts of machetes, beads, and mirrors on the Indians below. Initially, some of the Waimirí-Atroarí chiefs accepted these gifts and tried to negotiate with Indian agents along the Manaus–Bôa Vista Road. Then, following a series of unsuccessful encounters, the Waimirí-Atroarí made it clear that they would rather die fighting than give up their remaining territory and lands.[9]

During the first months of 1974, the Waimirí-Atroarí launched four attacks, killing more than fifteen Indian agents and

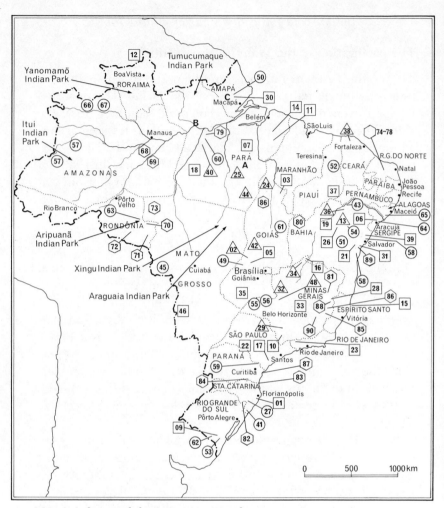

Map 4. Indians and the Amazon mining frontier
Source: Engineering and Mining Journal (November 1975), pp. 170–1.

Key: Multinational mining projects in the Amazon Basin:
A *Amazonia Mineração* (iron ore, Serra dos Carajas): $3 billion (American) project of U.S. Steel Corporation and Companhia Vale do Rio Doce to begin in 1980.
B *Mineração Rio do Norte* (bauxite, Trombetas River): $260 million project of Alcan Aluminum Company and Companhia Vale do Rio Doce to begin in 1977.
C *Industria e Comercio de Minerios* (manganese, Serra do Navio): large manganese mining and processing project of Bethlehem Steel Corporation and Cia. Auxiliar de Empresas Mineração began in 1957.

Map 4. Key (*cont.*): Mineral exploration projects being carried out by the Mineral
Resources Research Company (CPRM):

☐ **Finished projects**
1 Morro da Fumaça (Fluorite)
3 Serra da Gangalha (Diamonds)
7 Transamazônica
5 Santa Fé (Nickel)
6 Carmopolis (Potassium, rock salt)
9 Bagé (Copper)
10 Poços de Caldas (Molybdenum)
11 Paragominas (Bauxite)
12 Serra do Mel (Molybdenum)
14 Rio Capim (Kaolin)
15 Plat. Continental (Rock salt, potassium, sulphur)
16 Montalvania (Silver, zinc, lead, fluorite)
17 Morro do Serrote (Phosphate)
18 Rio Jamanxim (Silver, zinc, copper, lead)
19 Xique Xique (Lead)
21 Brasileia (Copper)
22 Cerro Azul (Niobium)
23 Morro Redondo (Bauxite)
26 Sacaiba (Chrome)
28 Aimores (Titanium)
30 Rio Falsino (Copper)
31 Itaparica (Limestone)
33 Alterosa (Limestone, beryllium)
35 Paraúna (Phosphate)
37 Massape (Vermiculite)
46 Corumbá (Iron)
39 Araçás (Coal)

△ **Projects under way**
2 Morro do Engenho (Nickel)
13 Andorinha (Chrome)
24 Arapoema (Nickel, copper)
25 São Felix do Xingu (Lead)
29 Catalão (Chrome)
32 Chaminés Alcalinas (Phosphate, diamonds, titanium, niobium)

34 Januaria-Itacarambi (Vanadium, silver, lead)
36 Curaçá (Copper)
38 Aprazivel (Copper)
40 Itamaguari (Gypsum)
42 Canadá (Copper)
44 Gradaus (Iron)
48 Patos de Minas (Phosphate)

○ **Projects awaiting a decision from DNPM**
27 Orleães (Coal)
41 Ararangua (Coal)
43 Tombador (Syenite)
45 Santa Barbara (Copper, chrome)
49 Bom Jardim (Lead, zinc)
50 Ita (Silver)
51 Ipirá (Chrome)
52 Pimenteiras (Phosphate)
53 Candiota (Coal)
54 Coite (Copper)
55 Três Ranchos (Niobium)
56 Ouvidor (Niobium)
57 Rio Jutaí (Lignite, peat, saprolite)
58 Ilheus (Phosphate)
59 Barra do Mendes (Nickel)
60 Aveiro (Limestone)
61 Dianópolis (Zinc)
62 Irui-Butia (Lignite)
63 Presidente Hermes (Iron)
64 São Cristovão (Phosphate, limestone, gypsum)
65 Propriá (Phosphate)
66 Uaupés (Titanium)
67 Tapuruquara (Titanium)

⬡ **1975 projects financed through CPRM**
68 Mineração Angelim SA (Cassiterite)

69 Concisa—Construção Civil e Industrial Ltda. (Cassiterite)
70 Progresso da Rondônia Mineração (Cassiterite)
71 Tin Brasil Mineração Ltda. (Cassiterite)
72 Mineração Aracazeiros Ltda. (Cassiterite)
73 Mineração Rio das Garças Ltda. (Cassiterite)
74 Mineração Amarante (Scheelite)
75 Mineração Tijuca Ltda. (Scheelite)
76 Mineração Acquarius (Scheelite)
77 Zangarelhas Mineração Ltda. (Scheelite)
78 Mineração Nordeste do Brasil Ltda. (Scheelite)
79 Camita SA (Rock salt)
80 Serrasa—Serra do Ramalho Mineração Ltda. (Fluorite)
81 Operadora de Equipamentos SA (Chromite)
82 Emp. Min. Imarui e Salomão Mineração Ltda. (Fluorite)
83 Leprevost e Cia. (Gold)
84 Mineração Morretes (Gold)
85 Minas Del Rei D. Pedro SA (Gold)
86 Mineração Morro Velho SA (Gold)
87 Eneel (Nickel)
88 C. R. Almeida SA (Ilmenite)
89 Somicol SA (Manganese)
90 Cia. Bozano Simonsen (Iron)

highway workers along the road. Finally, on December 27, 1974, an event occurred that highlighted all the problems facing FUNAI agents in this part of the Amazon Basin. On that day, thirty Waimirí-Atroarí tribesmen, led by a chief named Maroaga, attacked the Abonari Indian Post and killed four Indian agents. Among those killed was Gilberto Pinto Figueiredo, the director of FUNAI operations in the northern Amazon region. In the days following this attack, the new president of FUNAI, General Ismarth de Araújo Oliveira, was forced to call a temporary halt to all pacification efforts along the Manaus–Bôa Vista Road.[10]

Not surprisingly, the Waimirí-Atroarí attack received a large amount of coverage in the international press. In several of these reports, FUNAI officials were described as being atonished at the Waimirí-Atroarí's hostility toward the building of the Manaus–Bôa Vista Road. A FUNAI official named José de Aguiar, for example, was quoted by the *New York Times* as saying:

None of us knows why this happened. Another chief, Comprido, had led the other three attacks last year and perhaps Maroaga, in order to maintain his supremacy, had killed a white chief – and for them, that could only be Gilberto.[11]

According to a second FUNAI official, João Américo Peret, the Waimirí-Atroarí attack was launched against government personnel because the Indians lacked the technological and military capabilities to face the heavy earthmoving machines that were being used to build the new roads. "The Indians," Peret was quoted as saying in a *Time* magazine report, "resent the speed and aggressiveness with which the road is being built, but since they can't confront the road-building machines, they take it out on FUNAI people."[12]

Several other observers in Brazil interpreted the hostility of the Waimirí-Atroarí in quite different terms. Orlando Villas Boas, for example, was quoted as saying that:

The Atroaris are the same as other Indians. They repel any invasion of their lands and protect their families. They kill because it is the only way they can stop the white man.[13]

A similar position was expressed by Father José Vicente Cesar, president of the Roman Catholic Indian Missionary Council in Brazil. Father Vicente noted that the National Indian Foundation often "makes contacts with the Indians, but lacks the follow-up to preserve these contacts." Most of the Indian agents in the northwestern part of the Amazon, he went on to note, did not even speak the languages of the people who they were supposed to contact and protect. According to Father Vicente, FUNAI, rather than the Waimirí-Atroarí, was to blame for the December 1974 attack. It should have convinced the federal government, he argued, to have rerouted the Manaus–Bôa Vista Road and should have demarcated and defended the Waimirí-Atroarí Indian Reserve.[14]

In January 1975, just a week following the Waimirí-Atroarí attack, the most bizarre incident occurred. At that time, another Indian agent, Sebastião Amancio, was nominated to replace the deceased Gilberto Pinto Figueiredo as the director of FUNAI pacification efforts along the Manaus–Bôa Vista Road. In the days following this appointment, Amancio held an interview with the Brazilian newspaper *O Globo* in which he said that he and other Indian agents were sick of FUNAI's "war without weapons." According to Amancio, the traditional pacification strategy of FUNAI had failed, and it was time to use more direct means, such as dynamite, grenades, tear gas, and bursts from submachine guns in order to give the Indians "a demonstration of the force of our civilization."[15]

Sebastião Amancio said that he would not use these weapons against the Indians, but that they needed to be taught a lesson. Leaving more gifts for the Waimirí-Atroarí, he claimed, would only give them the idea that they were being rewarded for their attacks and killings of the past years. Instead, Amancio described how he would move into the Waimirí-Atroarí territory and build a large fortress at the Abonari Indian Post. This fortress, he went on to say, would have only one entrance, and a ladder that could be raised in case of attack. It would be stocked with dynamite, rockets, gas bombs, and grenades. This show of force, he told the press, would drive the Indians out of hiding and open up the area for the building of the road.

Amancio's bizarre plan shocked the Brazilian press, and after its announcement, several journalists called upon the president of FUNAI to make a statement about what official government policy would be like along the Manaus–Bôa Vista Road. Finally, on January 8, 1975, President Ismarth de Araújo Oliveira of FUNAI held a press interview in Brasília to discuss Indian policy in the Waimirí-Atroarí area. Ismarth de Araújo Oliveira said that Sebastião Amancio's views did not represent those of the Indian Foundation and that the Indian agent would be suspended pending an investigation of his remarks. At the same time, however, he admitted that FUNAI had reached an impasse in its numerous attempts to pacify the Waimirí-Atroarí tribe and that the Indians were "intransigently defending their lands." FUNAI, he claimed, was reevaluating its pacification strategy along the Manaus–Bôa Vista Road and was calling upon outside anthropologists and experienced Indian agents to develop a new plan to make peaceful contact with the tribe.[16]

A month later, in February 1975, FUNAI announced that it would resume its pacification efforts along the Manaus–Bôa Vista Road. At that time, Apoena Meirelles, the young Indian agent who had formerly directed operations in the Aripuanã Indian Park, was nominated to carry out the pacification of the Waimirí-Atroarí. According to the new plan, Meirelles would organize an eighty-member expedition team to make contact with the Waimirí-Atroarí. Fifty of these expedition members would serve as guards. The other thirty, led by Meirelles, would place gifts in front of the Waimirí-Atroarí villages and attempt to regain the confidence of the tribe. The road-building project, however, would continue as planned.[17]

In 1975, FUNAI also began to carry out another major pacification effort to the north and west of the Waimirí-Atroarí front in the Brazilian Territory of Roraima. One of the largest Indian groups in this region was the Yanomamö tribe, who were estimated to number between 10,000 and 15,000 and who lived in hundreds of isolated villages skirting the borders between Venezuela and Brazil. It is instructive to retrace our narrative somewhat and consider how these people have also been affected by new highway and development projects in the northern part of Brazil.

The situation of the Yanomamö tribe

The Yanomamö (also referred to as the Yanoama, Shirianá, Xirianá, Guaharibo, and Waiká) are the largest unacculturated Indian tribe in South America. For nearly a century, the Yanomamö were forced to retreat defensively into their present territory between the Orinoco River in Venezuela and the Marauia River in Brazil. To the south, they were attacked by Brazilian rubber collectors and settlers. To the north, they fought off the expanding cattle frontier in Venezuela, and the more acculturated and rifle-bearing Makiritare tribe. For at least two decades, metal tools and shotguns were introduced on the frontiers of Yanomamö territory, and passed inward, through exchange, to more isolated groups. North American evangelical missionaries and Italian Catholic priests began to enter the Yanomamö area in the early 1950s. By the early 1960s, the first reports began to appear about malaria and measles epidemics among the Yanomamö tribe.[18]

In August 1972, the four-member investigating team of the Aborigines Protection Society of London (APS) visited several Yanomamö communities located in the Brazilian Territory of Roraima. Initially, the APS team was impressed by the situation of the Yanomamö relative to other Indian groups in Brazil. Contacts with outsiders had only begun in the previous decade, and the Indians, according to the APS team, were "still largely insulated from the colonizing and commercial interests of Brazil."

The main contacts of the Yanomamö during this period were with foreign missionaries, who had established several mission stations in the area, but who seemed to pose little threat to the integrity of the tribe. "The Yanomamö," the APS team wrote in their 1973 report, "seemed to be content with their culture, and had proved strong enough to resist the converting zeal of missionaries."[19]

The APS team was also impressed by the fact that FUNAI was planning to intervene in this area. In the previous year, for example, a special reserve had been decreed for the Yanomamö tribe. To the surprise of the APS team, however, it was discovered that this proposed reserve would contain an area sufficient for only 300 members of the tribe and that it would exclude almost every Yanomamö village identified by FUNAI.

In their report, the APS team noted that none of the experienced missionaries in the Yanomamö area had been consulted about the boundaries of this reserve. Further, the APS team questioned whether the proposed limits of this reserve would endanger the tribe and suggested that negotiations be arranged with Venezuela for the establishment of an international Yanomamö reserve. "We consider," the APS team wrote in 1973, "that a major extension of this Reserve is both necessary and justified and furthermore that discussions should be opened with the Venezuelan authorities to see what forms of liaison and coordination of Indian policy are possible along the frontier."[20]

Since the publication of the APS report, FUNAI has taken a more active role in the Yanomamö area. At the same time, however, three events have occurred in this region that have stifled the development of an effective Indian policy and posed a critical threat to the continuing existence of the Yanomamö tribe.

First, over the past few years, the Brazilian government has begun to build a series of new roads through isolated parts of the Territory of Roraima. In May 1974, Edwin Brooks, a member of the APS team, published an article indicating how this new highway network would affect the Yanomamö tribe. Brooks's article contained a series of recent maps that showed that two new highways were being planned to pass through the proposed Yanomamö reserve. One of these highways, along the southern border of the reserve, was a section of the 2,500-mile Northern Perimeter Highway. The other was a smaller territorial road, which would cut across the northern part of the reserve and connect the mission stations at Catrimani and Surucucus. Both these highways, Brooks claimed, would jeopardize the territorial integrity of the Yanomamö tribe (see Map 3, Inset A).[21]

Second, in February 1975, the Brazilian minister of mines and energy, Shigeaki Ueki, announced that an immense uranium field had been discovered in the Surucucus region of Roraima. This area was one of the major locations of the Yanomamö tribe. According to one report, there were sixteen Yanomamö villages in the Surucucus region with a population of over 2,000. Until recently, the major agency providing assistance to these Indians was the Evangelical Mission Society of Amazonia (MEVA), staffed by two missionaries, one from Brazil and the other from the United States.

Actually, the existence of radioactive materials in this region was known as far back as 1951, but real uranium exploration did not begin until 1970, when the Brazilian government allocated large amounts of money for the mineral and nuclear sectors in Brazil. By 1974, over 150 technicians were working in the Surucucus region of Roraima alone, including members of the Brazilian military, Project Radam, the Mineral Resources Research Company, and Nuclebrás, the new state-owned company created to promote nuclear research in Brazil.[22]

Finally, throughout 1974 and 1975, a number of reports appeared that described the discovery of several new foci of the dreaded disease onchocerciasis (African river blindness) throughout the northwestern part of the Amazon Basin. Onchocerciasis is carried by a tiny blackfly of the Simuliid family, and is usually found close to riverine communities where the dangerous blackfly populations lay their eggs. To date, the most serious incidence of onchocerciasis has occurred in the seven countries along the Volta River basin in West Africa. About 1 million people have the disease in this area. Of these, about 70,000 are blind and over 30,000 see only poorly.[23]

In 1974, two American scientists, Robert J. A. Goodland and Howard S. Irwin, reported on the growing incidence of onchocerciasis in the Amazon Basin and cautioned the Brazilian government against building the Northern Perimeter Highway as planned. According to these scientists, a close relationship existed between deforestation activities associated with the Amazon highway construction program and the rapid spread of the dangerous blackfly population. Onchocerciasis, Goodland and Irwin claimed, was possibly the most serious health threat in the Amazon and was actively spreading along the margins of the Northern Perimeter Highway. "If the road planned to pierce the main focus is not realigned," they wrote, "disaster as rife as in Africa must be expected."[24]

Unfortunately, a FUNAI medical report of February 1975 confirmed these predictions. According to this report, onchocerciasis, which was previously localized in the area surrounding the Venezuelan frontier, had now spread beyond Roraima and was moving as far south as Pará, Acre, and the Center-West of Brazil. In the state of Amazonas alone, of a sample of 310 people investigated by the FUNAI medical team, 94 people, or nearly 30 percent, were found to be infected with the disease.

The most serious incidence of onchocerciasis had occurred among the Indian tribes of the northwestern part of the Amazon Basin. Along the Marauia River, one band of Yanomamö Indians was found to have a 100 percent index of the disease. In the Upper Solimões region, the Tikúna tribe had a positive index of 87.5 percent. Along the Damini and Mapalau rivers, five Indian tribes were all reported to have been infected. Lower indices of onchocerciasis were found among the Tucano and Makú tribes of the Uaupés River and among the Baníwa tribe of the Içana River region.

In revealing these statistics to the Brazilian press, President Ismarth de Araújo Oliveira claimed that the control of onchocerciasis was extremely difficult. He asserted that it would involve the intervention of several ministries and necessitate the expensive movement of people engaged in development projects along the Northern Perimeter Highway. Ismarth de Araújo Oliveira described the onchocerciasis epidemic as virtually "flying on the wings of the fly." The only combatant, he said, was an expensive French remedy which, when applied to Indians, supposedly killed them because of lack of physical resistance.[25]

Following the announcement of this epidemic, the Brazilian press increasingly looked for some official statement of what FUNAI policy would be in the Territory of Roraima. In a certain sense, the discovery of vast mineral deposits in this region provided a test case for evaluating the future direction of Indian policy in Brazil. Finally, in March 1975, the governor of Roraima, General Fernando Ramos Pereira, expressed his views on this question before the Brazilian press. "I am of the opinion," he said, "that an area as rich as this – with gold, diamonds, and uranium – cannot afford the luxury of conserving a half a dozen Indian tribes who are holding back the development of Brazil."[26]

On the day following this statement, the president of FUNAI held an interview in which he tried to clarify what Indian policy would be in the Territory of Roraima. In contrast to the governor's statement, President Ismarth de Araújo Oliveira claimed that there was nothing contradictory between the protection of the Indian tribes of Roraima, such as the large Yanomamö tribe, and the progress and development of Brazil. Citing Article 45 of the new Brazilian Indian Statute, which gives FUNAI the right to administer and lease Indian mineral resources, the president said that "the Indian can only benefit from the mineral wealth discovered on the lands which he inhabits." The Indian Statute, he pointed out, called for the "integration" of Indians into the Brazilian economy, and provides for their "participation," as owners of property, in the exploitation of mineral resources contained on their lands.

At the same time, the president revealed that a contract had been signed with two anthropologists associated with the University of Brasília for the creation of Project Perimetral-Yanomamö, a far-reaching government program for the integration of the Yanomamö tribe. The purpose of this project would be to set the groundwork for the eventual economic integration of the Yanomamö tribe into the colonization fronts in the far northern part of Brazil. The Indians, according to the president, would be inoculated against disease and provided with new economic skills in order to trade the products of their labor with colonists along the Northern Perimeter Highway. The philosophy behind this project, one of the anthropologists contracted by FUNAI was quoted as saying, was "to implant a system of *direct integration* [emphasis mine] that would permit economic advantages for both groups."[27]

During the past year, three more events have occurred that have a direct bearing on the future of the Yanomamö tribe. The first event was the signing of an important bilateral agreement between Brazil and West Germany for the provision of long-term supplies of natural uranium in exchange for the most advanced nuclear technology. Included in this agreement were plans for the construction of eight nuclear power plants in Brazil, the expansion of present uranium exploration activities, and the construction of a uranium enrichment and nuclear fuel recycling plant. From the point of view of the Yanomamö, this agreement probably signifies that the Brazilian government will soon begin to exploit the large uranium deposits discovered in Surucucus.[28]

The second event was the decision of both the Brazilian and Venezuelan governments to close off the Yanomamö area to investigations by foreign anthropologists. In essence, this decision cuts off all communication between the Yanomamö and foreign scholars and thus inhibits information from reaching the outside world on the situation of the tribe. In the case of Brazil, this decision was based on the argument that no foreigners are allowed by law to reside within a certain distance of the Brazilian frontier.[29]

Finally, it has recently been revealed that large deposits of cassiterite, as well as uranium, have been discovered in Yanomamö territory. Seemingly, since 1975, a major cassiterite boom has been taking place in the Territory of Roraima. According to one report, the governor of Roraima has given a mining company named Além-Equador exclusive rights to prospect for minerals in the hills surrounding the mission station at Surucucus and a landing strip has been built to carry out the minerals. Some reports indicate that both FUNAI and the Brazilian military have intervened to stop such unauthorized mineral exploration, but as of July 1976, a "climate of tension" was still reported to exist between prospectors and Indians in the area.[30]

The institutional context of Indian policy in Brazil

In March 1974, when General Ismarth de Araújo Oliveira became the new president of FUNAI, a number of observers hoped that there would be a basic change in Indian policy in Brazil. In certain respects, there was a basis for these hopes. One of the first acts of the new president, for example, was to attend a meeting of tribal chiefs in the Xingu National Park. At the same time, FUNAI called upon a number of anthropologists to serve in a consultative capacity with the agency and turned a sensitive ear to the criticisms of various dedicated Indian agents in Brazil. With reason, a number of former critics of the agency were impressed by the new openness of the FUNAI regime.

This enthusiastic response to the new FUNAI regime, however, tended to obscure the institutional context in which Indian policy has been forced to function in Brazil over the past several years. As I have tried to show in the preceding pages, FUNAI is an agency within the Brazilian Ministry of the Interior and hence has been substantially constrained, even under new leadership and direction, by the larger economic development program of the Brazilian military regime. Nowhere are these institutional constraints more clear than in those sections of the new Brazilian

Indian Statute that deal with the vital question of Indian land rights and that the new president of FUNAI cited in his response to the governor of Roraima in March 1975.

The Brazilian Indian Statute became law in December 1973, and has since served as the basic legislative mandate for the program of FUNAI. Certain sections of this new law (Title III, Chapter 1, Articles 17, 18, and 19) recognize the exclusive rights of Indian communities to territories and lands, and specifically define FUNAI's obligation to demarcate a series of Indian parks, territories, farming settlements, and reserves. In addition, this law explicitly states that "native land cannot be the object of leasing or renting or any juridical act or negotiation that restricts the *full exercise of direct possession* [emphasis mine] by the native community or forest-dweller."[31]

Several other articles in the same statute, however, directly contradict these provisions and claims, and provide a substantial threat to the territorial integrity of Indian tribes. Article 20, for example, states that the federal government can intervene in a native area and relocate tribal groups under six conditions. Two of these conditions are "to carry out public works [i.e., highways] of interest to national development," and "to work valuable subsoil deposits [i.e., minerals] of outstanding interest for national security and development."

Of equal, if not greater significance, is Title IV of the new statute, called "Assets and Income of the Indian Estate," which provides FUNAI with the right to administer and lease the resources contained on Indian lands. According to this title, Indian resources are conceived as part of the so-called Indian Estate, the "assets" of which are intended, through their rational management, investment, and exploitation, to generate "income" for Indian tribes.

Articles 39 through 42 of this title specifically define these "assets," and provide FUNAI with the right to manage and administer them. Article 43 gives FUNAI the right to reinvest these "assets . . . preferably in profitable activities, or . . . in Indian assistance programs." Finally, Articles 44 and 45 distinguish between ground and subsoil wealth, and provide the Brazilian Ministry of the Interior, through FUNAI, with the right to grant authorization to third parties for the purpose of leasing Indian mineral reserves.

These resource-management and -leasing provisions in the new Brazilian Indian Statute are perhaps the clearest reflection of how Brazilian Indian policy has become institutionally compromised with the wider economic development interests of the Brazilian military regime. These provisions run counter to the sentiment expressed in Article 198 of the Brazilian Constitution and contradict the entire protectionist history of Brazilian Indianist law. In essence, they provide a legal mandate for FUNAI to lease the strategic subsistence resources contained on Indian lands to powerful multinational and state-owned mining, timber, and agribusiness firms.

For anyone familiar with the history of Indian policy in other countries of the Americas, it is clear that the Brazilian government is attempting to institutionalize a type of Indian policy similar to that practiced in the United States. Despite a vast body of positive Indian law and hundreds of "sacred" international treaties, for nearly a century the U.S. Bureau of Indian Affairs has been leasing Indian mineral resources, waters, and lands. Ostensibly, this leasing policy is to provide monies for "Indian Treasuries" and to serve as the basis for financing programs that will acculturate Indian tribes. In point of fact, however, this policy has been one of the main reasons for the continual and unrelenting expropriation of Indian lands. Between 1887 and 1966, for example, the American Indian land base in the United States decreased from 138 million to 55 million acres. Without a major change in policy, and given the vast amount of economic activity now taking place in the Amazon Basin, one can only predict that the same fate awaits the remaining Indian tribes of Brazil.[32]

Part three

The social and ecological effects of the Polamazônia Program

1975 to 1979

8

The rise of agribusiness in Brazil

The vast grazing ranges of Central Brazil, Mato Grosso, and the Amazon Basin make it likely that Brazil will be the largest cattle producing country in the world in a relatively short period. FAO technicians believe that within 7 to 10 years Brazil can earn around $US 800 million annually by exporting meat, which will bring this product up to first or second place in the list of Brazilian exports.
"Food: Still the Leading Export," *Brazilian Trends*, 1972

Development experience in other countries and regions shows that cattle breeding can be an excellent way of settling in new areas, since cattle ranches are generally followed by commercial centers of growing importance. It is therefore possible that this occupation pattern will become the stable driving force behind the regional economy, since in Amazonia it appears to offer the greatest potential.
"Amazonia is Developing in Every Direction," *Brazilian Bulletin*, August 1974

When General Ernesto Geisel became the president of Brazil in March 1974, the Brazilian government was faced with the very important policy decision of choosing between two opposing models for the agricultural occupation and settlement of the Amazon. The first of these models was represented by the Institute for Colonization and Agrarian Reform (INCRA) colonization program along the margins of the Trans-Amazon Highway. As discussed in Chapter 3, this model included the resettlement of landless peasants from the Northeast to the Amazon, the provision of these colonists with small parcels of land and agricultural credit, and the production of basic subsistence crops such as rice,

111

beans, manioc, and corn. In contrast, the second model, which dated back to the years immediately following the military coup of 1964, provided for the establishment of large cattle ranches in the Amazon stimulated by fiscal and tax incentives from the state. This model called for the input of large sums of money from industrialists and agribusinessmen in the southern part of Brazil and looked toward the production of beef for world markets. By 1970, a major impetus in the direction of the establishment of such cattle ranches was already taking place in the central regions of Brazil.

In early 1974, the first indications began to appear that this second model would become the basic pattern for the occupation of the Amazon. At that time, reports coming out of Brazil revealed that the Brazilian government was deemphasizing its peasant colonization program along the margins of the Trans-Amazon Highway and giving major support to the large-scale cattle-ranching projects that had already been established in central Brazil. "The pretense of implementing reforms in the Northeast which would alleviate the misery of millions of subsistence farmers," the British weekly *Latin America* reported in May 1974, "is finally being abandoned in favor of large-scale agribusiness in Brazil."[1]

In September 1974, the government further clarified its position on the vital question of agrarian policy in the Amazon. At that time, President Geisel announced that the government would be creating a new project, called the *Polamazônia* Program, which would designate fifteen "poles of development" in the Amazon for the purposes of stimulating a series of new cattle-raising, timber, and mining ventures. "The moment has in effect arrived," a government report on the *Polamazônia* Program declared, "to take advantage of the potential represented by the Amazon, mainly to bring a significant contribution to raising the gross national product."[2]

The new *Polamazônia* Program was a second-stage proposal for the development of the Amazon, equal in scope to the Plan for National Integration (PIN) announced by then-President Médici in June 1970. The Bank of the Amazon, for example, was expected to budget over $1 billion (American billion) for Amazon development loans between 1975 and 1979, including nearly $500 million for cattle-raising projects. Over the same period, the Superintendency for the Development of the Amazon (SUDAM) predicted that more than $4 billion in private capital would be invested in the Amazon.

Most surprising, even INCRA, the agency specifically set up to resolve the problems of landless migrants from the Northeast, announced its support of the agroindustrial model of Amazon development. In the next five years, INCRA was preparing to sell over 52 million acres of public lands in the Amazon to large cattle-raising and timber enterprises. Some of these new projects would contain up to 178,000 acres of land.[3]

In this chapter, I shall assess some of the social implications of the rise of agribusiness in the Amazon region of Brazil. I shall begin with a description of the situation of Indians along the expanding Amazon cattle frontier. I shall then turn to a discussion of the effects that cattle ranching has had on the large peasant populations in the Amazon. Finally, I shall analyze the important role that multinational corporations and international lending institutions have assumed in the recent growth of agribusiness in Brazil.

Indians and the Amazon cattle frontier

Over the past decade, a major cattle-ranching frontier has been forming in the counties of Barra do Garças and Luciara in the Mato Grosso region of Central Brazil. For nearly a century, this immense region between the Araguaia and Xingu rivers was closed to Brazilian settlement because of attacks by Gê-speaking Xavante Indians. Then, in 1946, the Brazilian Indian Protection Service (SPI) pacified the Xavante, and a steady stream of settlers began to move into the area. The building of the Belém–Brasília

Highway speeded up this wave of internal migration, and, in the 1960s, a number of large corporations from southern Brazil began to claim land under the fiscal-incentives program of SUDAM. By the early 1970s, more than 60,000 people lived in Barra do Garças and Luciara, the majority of whom were subsistence farmers, agricultural workers, and remnants of the Xavante, Karajá, and Tapirapé tribes.[4]

By 1970, this part of Mato Grosso was one of the major cattle-raising areas of Brazil. In southern Brazil, for example, the average size of cattle ranches was only 800 to 900 hectares of land, and the largest ranch covered only 6,000. In Barra do Garças and Luciara, the immense Suiá-Missú Ranch alone covered 695,843 hectares.

Between 1966 and 1970, SUDAM approved sixty-six agri-business projects in the counties of Barra do Garças and Luciara (see Table 2). Among the investors in this area were the largest meat-packing firm in Brazil, the owner of the largest bus company in São Paulo, the president of the National Bank of Minas Gerais, the large Eletro-Radiobráz electronics firm, and David Nasser, one of Brazil's best-known television news reporters. At the end of 1970, the amount of fiscal incentives invested in these two counties alone totaled nearly 300 million Brazilian cruzeiros (Cr$).[5]

In October 1971, the Bishop of São Félix in Mato Grosso, Father Pedro Casaldáliga, issued an urgent document entitled *Uma Igreja da Amazônia em Conflito com o Latifúndio e a Marginalização Social* ("An Amazon Church in Conflict With Latifundia and Social Marginality"). Father Casaldáliga's report described the numerous conflicts created by this new cattle frontier. According to this report, the major groups affected by these cattle ranches were the several Indian tribes who lived in Barra do Garças and Luciara.

Under pressure from the ranch owners, the government had recently built two new highways through the northern part of this region, one of which traversed the northern section of the Xingu

Table 2. *Cattle-ranching projects approved by SUDAM in the counties of Barra do Garças and Luciara, Mato Grosso, Brazil, through 1970*

Name of ranch	Approximate area (ha)	Fiscal incentives (Cr$)
Agro-Pecuária Suiá Missú	695,843	7,878,000
Cia. de Desenvolvimento do Araguaia (CODEARA)	196,497	16,066,900
Agropecuária do Araguaia (AGROPASA)	48,165	7,122,208
Tapiraguaia Agrícola e Pecuária	21,923	2,519,404
Colonização e Representação do Brasil (COREBRASA)	52,272	3,130,000
Agropecuária São Francisco do Xingu	21,000	3,921,364
Agropecuária Guanabara	25,800	4,398,889
Agro-Pecuária São José	19,915	4,960,318
Agropecuária "Santa Rosa"	19,360	3,968,033
Agro-Pastoril Nova Patrocínio ("Fazenda Porta da Amazônia")	26,817	3,083,467
Agro Pecuária Tapirapé ("Fazenda Tapirapé")	27,614	3,109,694
Buritizal Agropecuária	30,621	3,939,638
Porto Velho Agropecuária	49,994	6,193,496
Agropecuária Foltran	13,741	3,319,720
Agro-Pecuária "Três Marias"	20,000	3,505,768
Tabaju Agro-Pecuária	19,931	3,019,474
Urupianga Agro-Pecuária	50,468	6,573,321
Rancho Santo Antonio	21,780	4,788,884
Pastoral Agro Pecuária Couto Magalhães	50,176	2,451,662
Agro Pecuária Duas Âncoras	23,005	4,191,575
Agro Pecuária "7 de Setembro Ltda."	18,582	2,025,620

115

Table 2 *(cont.)*

Name of ranch	Approximate area (ha)	Fiscal incentives (Cr$)
Agro Pecuária Médio Araguaia (AGROPEMA)	11,370	1,487,426
Cia. Agro Pastoril Sul da Amazônia	24,200	4,288,877
Joaçaba Agro-Pecuária	9,744	1,417,255
Cia. de Desenvolvimento Agro-Pecuário de Mato Grosso (CODEMA)	26,824	2,342,725
Empresa Agropecuária Ema	8,952	1,514,838
Agropecuária Alvorada Matogrossense (APAME)	29,703	4,332,496
Santa Luzia Agropecuária	4,930	1,959,037
União Gaucha Colonizadora Agropecuária (SOGUACHA)	26,300	5,247,075
Fazenda Tanguro Agro-Pecuária	33,562	2,149,072
Agropecuária Santa Silvia	39,574	3,028,000
Fazenda Nova Viena	29,503	4,718,377
Sociedade Agropecuária do Vale do Araguaia (SAPEVA)	72,567	6,208,686
Agropecuária California Comércio e Indústria (AGROINSA)	29,831	3,142,165
Agropecuária Duas Pontes	—	812,719
Agropecuária Nova Amazonia (FRENOVA)	—	4,872,318
Agropecuária Cocal	—	4,235,909
Curuá Agropecuária	9,455	1,432,258
Noidori Agropecuária	—	2,663,771
Elagro Pecuária	29,446	6,459,426
Pabreulândia Agro-Pastoril do Brasil Central	—	1,913,721
Nativa Agropecuária	—	1,593,654
Fazenda Nova Kênia	—	2,115,148
Agropecuária Brasil Novo	27,905	6,010,081
Agropecuária Planalto (AGROPLASA)	—	4,405,941

Table 2 (*cont.*)

Name of ranch	Approximate area (ha)	Fiscal incentives (Cr$)
Agropastoril Barra do Garças	9,998	4,784,430
Agropecuária Tamakavy	24,999	5,144,623
Agropecuária Roncador	24,251	5,379,188
Agropecuária Colorado	5,413	1,526,140
Fazendas Associadas do Araguaia (FAASA)	10,000	1,413,288
Agropecuária São João da Liberdade	—	6,213,140
Agropecuária Rio Manso	—	2,307,809
Cia. Agrícola e Pastoril S. Judas Tadeu	—	5,955,380
Rio Fontoura Agropecuária	14,864	3,754,920
Tracajá Agropecuária	29,880	3,798,133
Independência Agropecuária	—	1,460,546
Sociedade Agropecuária Brasil Central	31,110	3,729,142
Agropecuária Tatuibi	19,936	5,973,970
Norte Pastorial Matogrossense	—	5,881,454
Companhia Agropecuária Sete Barras	19,360	6,320,477
Companhia de Desenvolvimento Garapu (CODESGA)	9,000	3,207,265
Agropastoril Campo Verde	64,819	6,565,129
Companhia Agropastoril Aruanã (CIAGRA)	—	5,975,784
Colonizadora e Representações Brasileiras (COLBRASA)	24,969	6,774,833
Agropecuária Bela Vista	36,125	4,390,924
Agropecuária Remanso Açu	—	2,989,015

Source: Pedro Casaldáliga, *Uma Igreja da Amazônia em Conflito com o Latifúndio e a Marginalização Social* (Mato Grosso, 1971), pp. 49–59.

National Park (see the discussion of the BR-080 Highway invasion in Chapter 4). At the time of this highway invasion, one of the ranch owners was quoted as saying, in reference to the potentially rich pasturage in this area, that the lands belonging to the Xingu National Park were the "filet mignon" of Brazil. In his report, Father Casaldáliga described how the Indians who had left the Xingu Park were in a state of disorganization and despair. "Without concrete and regular assistance," he wrote, "and without well-defined lands, these peoples arrive at the highways, stopping trucks and buses, and begging for food."[6]

Similar conditions faced other tribes in this part of Mato Grosso. To the north of the Xingu National Park, for example, a large ranch had laid claim to lands belonging to the Tapirapé tribe. To the east, on the Ilha do Bananal, a town of 5,000 Brazilian settlers and a herd of over 200,000 head of cattle had been established on the lands of the Karajá tribe (see Map 3, Inset B).

In 1971, Robin Hanbury-Tenison of Survival International in London visited this area of Mato Grosso. Hanbury-Tenison reported that almost all the Indian tribes in this area who were outside of the Xingu National Park were suffering from hunger and disease as a result of cattle invasions into their traditional hunting territories. "The prime necessity," he wrote, "is to introduce meat into the diet to replace the waning supply of game."[7]

During this period, the most severe conflicts were taking place between cattle ranchers and the Xavante tribe. Following the pacification of the Xavante in 1946, the Brazilian government promised to create a reserve for the tribe. For a brief period, it appeared as if this promise would be fulfilled, and at least one governor of Mato Grosso did guarantee the Xavante temporary title to their lands. Then in the 1950s several governors began to sell the Xavante lands, and in the early 1960s the new cattle ranchers began to arrive.

When the large Suiá-Missú Ranch was approved by SUDAM, a group of Xavante numbering 263 people were living on its lands. In 1966, the owner of the Suiá-Missú Ranch, Orlando Ometo, commissioned a Brazilian Air Force (FAB) plane to transfer the Indians to a Salesian mission station at a place called São Marcos to the south. A few days after their arrival at São Marcos, a fatal measles epidemic struck this band of the Xavante tribe. Eighty-three Xavante died at this time.[8]

Throughout the late 1960s, tensions continued to grow between the Xavante and the new cattle ranchers in their midst. In 1970, the Brazilian government attempted to resolve these tensions by promising to create a series of reserves for the Xavante tribe. These promises, however, again proved empty, and, in 1971, the Xavante decided to take the situation into their own hands. Under the leadership of a number of chiefs, the Xavante began to kill cattle and burn the houses of ranchers who had invaded their lands. Finally, in 1972, the government called a state of emergency in the Xavante area and sent a contingent of military police to the region to control conflicts between the ranchers and the Indians.[9]

At this time, a state of generalized economic euphoria was engulfing the town of Barra do Garças as a result of the recent cattle boom. Land prices in the area surrounding the town had risen tenfold in the past three years. Two new refrigerated meat plants had been built in the town. Nearly 2,000 head of cattle were being slaughtered every day. Most important, the cattle ranchers wanted to insure that the federal government did not survey the Xavante lands. "These Indians," one rancher was quoted as saying in the Brazilian press, "are holding back the inevitable development of Brazil. They produce absolutely nothing and are creating conflicts with pioneers who want to integrate our country and make it the major exporter of meat in the world."[10]

In September 1972, the Brazilian government made another attempt to clarify the land-tenure situation in this part of Mato Grosso. On September 14, 1972, the president of Brazil signed two decrees calling for the creation of Indian reserves in the Xavante communities of Sangradouro and São Marcos. Five days later, the president signed another decree creating three more Xavante reserves in the communities of Areões, Pimentel Barbosa, and Couto Magalhães.[11]

Despite these measures, conflicts continued to occur between the ranchers and the Indians. In March 1973, for example, bitter clashes broke out between cattle ranchers and Xavante Indians at the Couto Magalhães Indian Reserve. The Indians on this reserve were outraged by the constant land invasions of the ranchers and by the inability of the federal government to demarcate their lands. "FUNAI," a Xavante chief from Couto Magalhães told the Brazilian press, "says that the Reserves are ours, but it has not demarcated these lands, and the ranchers will not leave them."[12]

Similar clashes occurred at the Sangradouro Reserve. In the summer of 1973, a government surveyor named João Pereira Evangelista attempted to survey the lands belonging to the Sangradouro Reserve. On arriving at the reserve, Evangelista was met by a group of armed ranchers who refused to let him measure the Xavante lands. The Indians were angered by these acts and attempted to provide protection for Evangelista in his work. In the end, however, Evangelista was able to measure only 84 of the 360 kilometers of land that were officially decreed for this community. In October 1973, the government was forced to call another state of emergency at the Sangradouro Reserve.[13]

To date, the most violent incidents have occurred between ranchers and Indians at the São Marcos Reserve. Over the past several years, a major physical and cultural revival has been taking place at this reserve. With the medical assistance of the Salesian Fathers, the population in the community has been increasing in size. A number of younger Indians have learned to speak Portuguese, and there has been a sense of vitality and hope in the São Marcos community.

In the early 1970s, however, a number of ranchers began to make claims to the lands of this community. Ten ranchers claimed that they possessed a title to the São Marcos Reserve and tried to petition the federal government to have the Indians removed. The Indians responded to these acts by killing the cattle of the invading ranchers and by blocking trucks that were seeking passage along a nearby road. Then, in August 1974, a group of armed ranchers attacked the Xavante of the São Marcos community and attempted to remove the Indians forcibly from their lands. The Indians were particularly angered by this incident because it occurred on the same day as an important ceremony for the adolescent boys of the tribe. In response, the Indians of São Marcos took up arms and again attempted to defend their lands. "We are the original owners of the land," one Xavante chief told a reporter at the time of the August 1974 incident, "and the ranchers have got to get off. They are not going to push us any more."[14]

At present, all five of the Xavante communities mentioned above remain without secure tenure to their lands. The situation of these communities represents the conditions that will inevitably face other Indian tribes who survive the first stages of contact with the expanding Brazilian economic frontiers. In essence, these tribes are powerless before the new cattle-ranching projects that are sprouting up throughout the Amazon and central regions of Brazil. Without effective legal protection from FUNAI, at any moment these tribes can be dispossessed of their lands.

Agrarian protest in Mato Grosso

Indian tribes such as the Xavante are only one among many groups of people who are being uprooted by the new Amazon cattle frontier. Over the past decade, for example, thousands of landless and unemployed peasants have been brought into Mato Grosso to clear lands for the new ranches and farms. In his report on social conditions in Barra do Garças and Luciara, Father Casaldáliga describes in detail the situation of this growing rural proletariat which is presently forming in the backland areas of central Brazil.

According to Father Casaldáliga, the majority of workers on the new cattle ranches come from Goiás and the Northeast of Brazil. The usual method of hiring these workers is for the cattle ranchers to send out labor contractors who are called *gatos* ("cats") in Portuguese. The labor contractors travel to the centers of rural unemployment in Brazil and promise workers that if they sign contracts they will be given good salaries, excellent working conditions, free medical assistance, and transportation to the farms. Most of these contracts are for a short period of time and stipulate that the workers will be able to leave once they fulfill their obligations of clearing the forests and lands.

On arriving at the ranches, however, the workers find an entirely different situation from that described in the contracts that they have signed. One of the first things they are told, for example, is that they must pay for their transportation and must purchase food and tools from the company store. Then the workers are loaded onto boats or into small airplanes and taken off to the jungle where they are to work.

Father Casaldáliga describes these jungle operations as "slave camps" where workers are forced to labor for long hours under the most miserable and oppressive conditions. There are no permanent houses in the jungle for these workers. Malaria is endemic. No medical assistance is provided by the ranchers. Most important, the heads of the jungle labor teams carry pistols and machine guns and use every form of terror to assure that the workers do not rebel or escape.

According to Father Casaldáliga, the owners of the cattle ranches in Barra do Garças and Luciara look upon these agricultural workers as an "inferior race." At present, Father Casaldáliga claims, there is a need for an abundant supply of such labor to clear the jungle and introduce pasturage for the new cattle herds. Once the ranches are established, however, these workers will again be displaced.[15]

Father Casaldáliga's report also describes the conditions of thousands of peasant small-holders (*posseiros*) who are being uprooted and dispossessed by the new ranches and farms. According to Father Casaldáliga, some of these peasants have been living in this region for as long as forty years. When these people first arrived in Mato Grosso, they were considered to be the heroic pioneers of the Brazilian interior. In exchange for their efforts, the Brazilian government provided these settlers with small village estates (*patrimônios*). At the time of the publication of Father Casaldáliga's report, there were five such peasant estates in Barra do Garças and Luciara named Santa Terezinha, Pôrto Alegre, Cedrolândria, Serra Nova, and Pontinópolis.

For a period of time, a situation of mutual tolerance existed between these peasant communities and the several Indian tribes in northern Mato Grosso. Then, in the late 1960s, the large cattle ranches arrived, and, like the Indians, the peasant small-holders were faced with the expropriation of their lands. From this time onward, there were frequent conflicts between the peasants and the new cattle ranches in their midst.[16]

One of the major peasant communities affected by the expansion of cattle ranching was the town of Santa Terezinha, located along the margins of the Araguaia River to the north of the Ilha do Bananal. In 1966, the Superintendency for the Development of the Amazon (SUDAM) authorized the creation of a large cattle-raising project in Santa Terezinha under the name of Companhia de Desenvolvimento do Araguaia (CODEARA). The CODEARA Ranch had an extension of 196,497 hectares and was registered under the names of three agribusinessmen from São Paulo, Armando Conde, Carlos Alves Seixas, and Luiz Gonzaga Murat.

At the time of the establishment of this ranch, there were more than 140 peasant families living in Santa Terezinha. Two schools existed in the community. The local Catholic church, under the direction of a French priest named Father François Jentel, maintained a primary school, a mobile health clinic, and a literacy program for adults. An agricultural cooperative had recently been formed to market peasant products and to represent the community before state and national authorities.

Beginning in 1967, the peasant community of Santa Terezinha, in collaboration with Father Jentel and various church officials in Mato Grosso, began an extensive campaign to obtain legal title to their lands. On April 12, 1967, for example, the people of Santa Terezinha submitted a long memorandum to the Brazilian minister of agriculture that described the precarious nature of the land-tenure situation in this community since the establishment of the CODEARA Ranch. This memorandum noted that on several occasions the administrators of the ranch had attempted to dispossess the peasants of their lands. It claimed that the authorities of Mato Grosso had refused to intervene in this situation and that the local military police had used terrorist tactics against the community. In addition, it noted that Father Jentel had personally talked with the directors of the CODEARA Ranch in São Paulo, but that he was unsuccessful in convincing them to respect the rights of the peasants to land.

To alleviate this situation, the peasant community of Santa Terezinha submitted its memorandum to the Brazilian minister of agriculture. This memorandum called upon the minister of agriculture to petition the president of Brazil to intervene in favor of the land claims of the community. Specifically, it asked for three things: (1) the creation of a district of Santa Terezinha, as an official administrative unit within the jurisdiction of the county of Luciara; (2) the concession of land titles to peasants living in Santa Terezinha in accord with a recent census carried out by the Brazilian Institute of Agrarian Reform (IBRA); and (3) the appropriation of an estate measuring 10,000 hectares for purposes of colonization, to be administered by the Cooperative of Santa Terezinha rather than the CODEARA firm. On November 29, 1967, Brazilian President Arthur Costa e Silva signed a decree authorizing IBRA to intervene in favor of the peasants of Santa Terezinha.[17]

For nearly two years, no action was taken on this decree, and it was not until October 1969 that IBRA finally decided in favor of the land rights of the peasants of Santa Terezinha and against the claims of the CODEARA firm. In the months following this decision, however, CODEARA began to use its political influence to reverse the decision of IBRA. Administrators of the ranch made several attempts on the lives of peasants in Santa Terezinha. The owners charged Father Jentel and Edival Pereira dos Reis, one of the peasant leaders of the community, with subversion. CODEARA attempted to convince various state and national officials to use their positions to support the land claims of the ranch. Finally, in May 1970, officials of IBRA cut off their support for the community of Santa Terezinha, and the peasants were left to face the CODEARA Ranch on their own.[18]

According to Father Casaldáliga, in October 1971 a "war of nerves" existed between peasants and ranchers in this part of Mato Grosso. Then, in February 1972, a group of administrators from the CODEARA Ranch attacked a number of peasants who were collaborating with Father Jentel in the building of a health clinic in Santa Terezinha. The administrators were aided by a tractor, which rammed through the walls of the new clinic, destroying the water well, the garden, and a large supply of costly construction materials. Father Jentel and his peasant followers denounced these acts before local and state authorities. No action, however, was taken to protect the peasants.

Finally, on March 3, 1972, the CODEARA men again arrived at the clinic. This time they were accompanied by a group of military police dressed in civilian clothing and armed with machine guns. Faced with the threat that their clinic would be taken by force, the peasant parishioners of Father Jentel took up arms and opened fire on the ranchers and police. Seven people were wounded in this incident, and the town of Santa Terezinha was placed under military control.[19]

In the months following this incident, the Brazilian government accused Father Jentel of responsibility for this attack, alleging that he had armed his parishioners with submachine guns. Church officials in Mato Grosso denied these accusations and claimed that the military government was using the case of Father Jentel to attack the growing number of priests who were supporting the just claims of peasants to their lands.

Father Jentel's trial began in May 1973 before one civilian and four military judges. In the course of this trial, the four military judges ignored the fact that the CODEARA firm, in collaboration with the local military police, had invaded church and peasant lands. During the trial, the government prosecutor accused Father Jentel of threatening the "national security" of Brazil and of attacking the legitimacy of the military regime.

In July 1973, the Brazilian tribunal, against the one dissenting vote of the civilian judge, sentenced Father Jentel to ten years imprisonment. Father Jentel remained in prison for a year and then was expelled from the country. Since this time, he has been denied permission to return to Brazil.[20]

Perhaps more than anyone else, the priests and bishops of the Amazon comprehend the depressing social reality faced by millions of rural peoples in modern-day Brazil. In his report on social conditions in Barra do Garças and Luciara, for example, Father Casaldáliga notes that if the incentives given to the oligarchies and trusts from the south of the country had been invested in the peasantry of the country, a very different set of events would have occurred in Mato Grosso in recent years. "Such investment," Father Casaldáliga writes, "could have produced a future of hope and development for all of these people in the interior of Brazil, rather than perpetuate the inequities of the latifúndia system which is socially and radically unjust."[21]

Multinational corporations and cattle ranching in the Amazon

Since the publication of Father Casaldáliga's report, an enormous growth has taken place in the scope of cattle-ranching activities in the Amazon Basin of Brazil. At least three international factors explain this phenomenal growth.

First, over the past few years, the Brazilian government has borrowed large sums of money from the World Bank and other international lending institutions for the purpose of expanding cattle ranching and the meat industries in Brazil. In 1972, for instance, the World Bank and the Inter-American Development Bank loaned the Brazilian government $86 million for the rehabilitation of existing meat-processing plants in the country and for the construction of several new plants in ten states. This was followed, in April 1974, by another loan of $60 million from the World Bank for purposes of improving cattle raising in Brazil.[22]

Both these loans were extremely important in raising the productivity of Brazilian livestock and in making credit available to Brazilian ranchers. At the same time, these loans stimulated the growth of meat-processing plants in the Amazon and central regions of Brazil.

In 1974, for example, the Swift-Armour Company of Brazil was planning to build two new meat-packing plants in Goiás and Pará. The Bordon Company was reequipping its meat-packing plant in the town of Anápolis, Goiás. The Anglo Company was purchasing equipment from Argentina for a new meat-packing plant in Goiánia. Comabra, a former subsidiary of the Wilson Meat Packing Company, was planning to build a new plant in Mato Grosso. "The production capacity for slaughtering and processing beef and pork," a U.S. Department of Commerce report on Brazil claimed in August 1974, "is expanding and being modernized to prepare for Brazil's entry into the world market in a really big way by 1977."[23]

A second important international factor that has sped up the growth of cattle ranching in the Amazon is the sudden inflation in world meat prices that occurred in the early 1970s. From December 1972 to March 1973, for example, the average price of beef in the United States rose from $1.15 to $1.35 per pound – an increase of 17 percent in just three months. At the same time, a sirloin steak selling for $1.69 per pound in the United States cost $1.88 per pound in England, $2.45 per pound in Belgium, and $2.79 per pound in Italy. In 1972, the United States alone imported two billion (American) pounds of beef – only 8 percent of total national consumption, but more than one-third of all beef traded on the international market.[24]

During this period, the Food and Agriculture Organization (FAO) of the United Nations estimated that by 1980 beef consumption outside the United States, particularly in Japan and the European Common Market countries, would be 37 percent above what it was in 1970. Not surprisingly, Brazil began to set its sights on becoming one of the largest beef producers and exporters in the world.[25]

In 1973, the Brazilian national cattle herd was estimated to number 90 million head, the third largest in the world and surpassed only by the herds of Russia and the United States. The potential for growth in the Brazilian cattle sector, however, surpassed every other nation in the world. Vast grazing lands still existed in the central and Amazon regions of Brazil. Present pasturage could be greatly improved. The large national herd was being poorly used. The domestic market for beef had a great potential for expansion. In 1973, meat exports from Brazil were valued at $400 million. By 1980, the Brazilian government hopes to double its meat production and become the major beef exporter in the world.[26]

The third and decisive factor in the rise of cattle ranching in the Amazon has been the great interest multinational corporations have shown in the region. One of the most-publicized foreign projects in the Amazon is the large Jari Forestry and Ranching Company owned by the multibillionaire shipping tycoon, Daniel Keith Ludwig, of the National Bulk Carriers Corporation in the United States. The Jari Forestry and Ranching Company covers a 3-million-acre area along the Jari River in the Brazilian Territory of Amapá. The estate was acquired by Ludwig in the late 1960s, and has since served as a model for other multinational agribusiness ventures in the Amazon.[27]

At present, more than 20,000 people live on this estate in Monte Dourado, a planned city created by Ludwig. The administrators of this estate, many of whom have had agricultural experience in the United States, have already cleared 250,000 acres of land and replanted it with two imported species of valuable commercial trees. At the same time, Ludwig has brought in 12,000 head of cattle from another ranch he owns in Venezuela and has set aside 5,000 acres for the creation of an experimental rice farm.

According to a recent *New York Times* article on the Jari Forestry and Ranching Company, the man who convinced Ludwig to invest in the Amazon was Roberto de Oliveira Campos, the former minister of planning in Brazil. Apparently, as far back as 1964 Campos traveled to New York to convince Ludwig and other American investors to set up large agribusiness projects in the Amazon. "Ludwig," Campos is quoted as saying, "is accustomed to investing in lunatic adventures, and just as accustomed to having them pay off. He has always been 15 years ahead of other entrepreneurs."[28]

Another multinational company that has recently invested in the Amazon is the Italian firm, Liquigas. Liquigas is a major producer of industrial chemicals in Brazil. In the early 1970s, Liquigas purchased a major share in the large Suiá-Missú Ranch in Mato Grosso. According to *Fortune* magazine, Liquigas was planning to expand the herd of 68,000 Zebu cows on the Suiá-Missú Ranch to 300,000 head, and to crossbreed them with Chianina and Marchigiana bulls imported from Italy. It was also reported to be building an airstrip on the ranch that would be big enough to land chartered jets. "The company," *Fortune* reporter Richard Armstrong wrote, "will slaughter on the ranch, package the meat in supermarket cuts with the price stamped on in lire, and fly it direct to Italy letting nature do the chilling job at 30,000 feet."[29]

Finally, to the north of the Suiá-Missú Ranch, the West German automobile manufacturer, Volkswagen, has recently purchased a large ranch. The Volkswagen Ranch is located in a place called Santana do Araguaia (southern Pará) and is reported to cover 56,000 acres. By 1982, Volkswagen plans to be grazing 110,000 head of cattle on this ranch and to be exporting beef to markets in Europe, Japan, and the United States. "We went into the cattle industry," a Volkswagen spokesman said, "for economic reasons and in answer to the government's appeal for large companies to participate in the development of the Amazon."[30]

Several important trends are reflected in these new cattle-ranching projects in the Amazon. First, a number of industrial firms located in the South of Brazil, such as Volkswagen, are investing in cattle ranching to take advantage of the fiscal and tax-incentives program of the Brazilian government. Second, some of these firms, such as Liquigas, are forming joint ventures with Brazilian agribusinessmen and hence playing an important role in the modernization of Brazilian agriculture. Finally, a process of vertical integration is taking place in Brazilian agriculture, linking up large-scale cattle ranching with the industrial processing and marketing of meats.

An excellent example of the above trends is provided by Deltec International Ltd., one of the largest private investment banks in the world. In 1969, Deltec Panamerica, the Latin American subsidiary of Deltec International, purchased International Packers Ltd. (IPL), one of the world's largest meat-packing firms. Through this purchase, Deltec gained control of IPL's holdings in the Swift-Armour Company of Brazil. At the time of this purchase, the Swift-Armour Company of Brazil was joining with the King Ranch of Texas to establish a 176,000-acre cattle ranch in the Amazon under the fiscal-incentives program of SUDAM. At the same time, Deltec began to lay plans for the construction of a large meat-processing plant on the Ilha de Marajó at the mouth of the Amazon River.[31]

By 1971, Deltec International was one of the largest producers and exporters of beef in Brazil. At the end of that year, approximately 30 percent of Brazilian beef exports were controlled by Deltec International and its Brazilian affiliates.

In 1972, Deltec sold its interests in the King Ranch project and in the Swift-Armour Company of Brazil to two close business associates – Brascan, a large Canadian investment company, and Cia. Auxiliar de Emprésas de Mineração (CAEMI), one of the largest and most powerful holding companies in Brazil. At the time of this sale, the *Wall Street Journal* reported that Deltec International had made an agreement with the new owners of its Brazilian companies to continue to distribute Swift-Armour Company of Brazil products in overseas markets.[32]

In November 1974, at the time of the World Food Conference in Rome, the Transnational Institute of Amsterdam issued a report entitled *World Hunger: Causes and Remedies*. This report noted that:

At present there is an increasingly strong trend on the part of multinational agribusiness companies to direct their control of resources in underdeveloped countries toward obtaining food products and raw materials for marketing operations in the developed world, without regard for the priority needs of the hungry in those countries.

The report continued:

The goal of the worldwide agribusiness firms is not feeding people but making profits. While tomorrow they might seek even greater profits in another industry, today their business is food. They find that the "real money" in food is in marketing food, produced as cheaply as possible in the most "sophisticated," wasteful, and ecologically destructive – but highly profitable – packaging to those relatively few in the world who have the money to pay for it.[33]

The Transnational Institute report on *World Hunger: Causes and Remedies* provides a basis for understanding the larger meaning of the recent cattle boom in the Amazon Basin of Brazil. Since the United Nations World Food Conference much attention has focused on the so-called world food crisis and the problems of hunger and malnutrition faced by the vast majority of people in the underdeveloped countries of the world. In the midst of this discussion, however, very few observers have ana-

lyzed the agrarian policies being carried out by national governments and being supported by international lending institutions
and multinational agribusiness firms.

In the previous pages, I have attempted to describe some of the
social consequences of national agrarian policy in the Amazon
region of Brazil. Beginning with the SUDAM fiscal-incentives
program in 1966, and increasingly since the announcement of
the new *Polamazônia* Program in 1974, the objectives of national
agrarian policy in the Brazilian Amazon have been twofold: (1) to
set the groundwork for the expansion of large domestic and multinational agribusiness corporations into the Amazon Basin; and
(2) to increase the export agricultural capacity of the Brazilian national economy.

In social terms, this policy has had three major consequences.
First, it has threatened the already precarious territorial integrity
of several Indian tribes in the Amazon, such as the Xavante tribe
in Mato Grosso. Second, it has increased the disparities between
land-poor and land-rich in rural Brazil, uprooting peasant small-
holders and creating a class of exploited agricultural workers. Finally, and perhaps most important of all, this policy, because of
its export orientation, has taken food away from the domestic
market and worsened the already severe pattern of hunger and
malnourishment that characterizes the majority of the population of Brazil.

Recent studies of infant mortality, the best indicator of a country's nutritional status, provide a clear picture of what the recent
"economic miracle" in agriculture has meant for the vast majority of Brazilians. Field studies by the World Health Organization, for example, indicate that 105 out of every 1,000 children
born in Brazil die during their first year of life. In Recife, the
major city in the Northeast, infant mortality rates are greater than
in any other city in Latin America. Government statistics show
that in some interior towns of the Northeast, infant mortality
rates are around 250 per 1,000 live births, and that for the Northeast as a whole the average infant mortality rate is 176 per 1,000

births. The northeastern region is estimated to have the seventh highest infant mortality rate in the world. Every minute, one child dies in the Brazilian Northeast.[34]

Similar figures exist for the city of São Paulo, the most modern and developed area of Brazil. In 1960, for example, the infant mortality rate in São Paulo stood at 77.17 per 1,000 live births. By 1970, following a decade of industrialization and economic growth, this figure rose to 83.64 deaths per 1,000 children born in the city.[35]

There is general agreement that the major reason for these high infant mortality rates is the inadequate diet of children in Brazil. A study begun in Recife in 1967, for example, led one investigator to conclude that "91 percent of the children who die before 5 years of age do so simply because of hunger."[36]

In a situation such as this, disease spreads rapidly, and even those who escape sickness or death in their first years of life are marked forever by the early childhood experience of malnutrition. A report by Dr. Dalva Sagey for the Brazilian Ministry of Education and Culture, for instance, concluded that "of the 20,855,800 children up to six years of age in Brazil, 8,234,350 (or 40 percent) have food shortages, and it is these deficiencies which cause brain damage, and will later be transformed into mental retardation."[37]

Malnutrition, though, is not a condition of only children in Brazil. A report published in 1973 found that even in the city of São Paulo over 60 percent of an adult population sample examined was undernourished. The lower-income group, which formed 60 percent of this sample and which earned less than 500 Brazilian cruzeiros per month, showed a 73.8 percent deficit in their necessary intake of Vitamin A and a 43.7 percent deficit in their intake of Vitamins B and C.

In August 1973, the London-based weekly *Latin America* carried an article titled, "Brazil: Rich Man, Poor Man." This article noted that one of the results of the "economic miracle" in Brazilian agriculture was to increase the disparities between rich and poor in Brazil. One of the main reasons for these disparities, this article claimed, was the export orientation of the Brazilian agricultural economy. "The poverty of the rural population," the article concluded, "stands out in ever-sharpening contrast to the industrial splendors of the economic miracle and there is every reason to suppose that the situation is getting worse."[38]

9

The deforestation of the Brazilian Amazon

They are turning the Amazon Basin into a desert, destroying its forests, rivers, and animal life, and there was nothing I could do to stop them. . . . I was born in the Northeastern state of Ceará at a place called Cedro where there's no green left, and I'm afraid they will transform the entire area from the shores of Ceará to central Amazonia into another Sahara.

> José Piquet Carneiro, former president of the Brazilian Foundation for the Conservation of Nature, quoted in "Conservationist Stirs Furor in Brazil," *New York Times*, June 2, 1974

The process of systematic destruction of native forest is a crime against the country. Our children will live in deserts unless measures that protect the environment from destruction become effective immediately.

> Roberto Burle Marx, Brazil's leading landscape architect, quoted in "Brazil Pushing Development of Amazon Despite Warnings," *Miami Herald*, January 6, 1975

Over the past several years, a number of eminent scientists throughout the world have criticized the potentially devastating ecological effects of the Brazilian government's program to occupy and exploit the Amazon Basin. These criticisms have ranged from a concern that the entire Amazon rain forest would be deforested in the coming decades to forecasts about the effects of such massive environmental destruction on the oxygen and carbon dioxide content of the earth's atmosphere. Recently, two American scientists, Robert J. A. Goodland of the Cary Arboretum (Millbrook, New York) and Howard S. Irwin of the New York Botanical Garden (Bronx, New York), have discussed these

135

issues in an exceptionally well-documented book entitled *Amazon Jungle: Green Hell to Red Desert?* Goodland and Irwin's study was originally published in the journal *Landscape Planning* in October 1974 under the title of "An Ecological Discussion of the Environmental Impact of the Highway Construction Program in the Amazon Basin." Along with other topics, Goodland and Irwin disputed the economic and ecological viability of the proposed Institute for Colonization and Agrarian Reform (INCRA) agricultural colonization program along the Trans-Amazon roads.[1]

Since the publication of this study, two important events have occurred that, at least from the viewpoint of the Brazilian government, have been looked upon as a direct response to various ecological criticisms of the Amazon development program. The first of these events, as mentioned in the previous chapter, was the announcement by officials of INCRA that the government was planning to deemphasize its program of peasant colonization along the Trans-Amazon Highway. According to INCRA officials, between October 1970 and January 1974 only 4,969 families had been settled along the Trans-Amazon Highway, a minuscule part of the 100,000 families that INCRA had officially claimed it would settle in the Amazon by 1975. As far back as 1973, in fact, INCRA had suspended all arrangements for colonists to arrive in the Amazon by plane, boat, and truck, and it was now merely providing assistance to those colonization projects that were already established in Altamira and Santarém.

This change in policy, INCRA officials claimed, resulted from two factors: (1) the failure of the first experiments in agricultural colonization along the Trans-Amazon Highway; and (2) the growing evidence provided by scientific and aerial-photographic surveys of poor soil properties in the Amazon. Government planners saw the termination of the INCRA colonization program as a response to ecological criticisms in recent years.[2]

The second event was the announcement by the Superintendency for the Development of the Amazon (SUDAM) that it was planning, as part of the *Polamazônia* Program, to rationalize and modernize all land-use practices in the Amazon Basin. In 1974, for example, SUDAM issued a detailed study entitled, *Estudos Básicos Para O Establecimento de Uma Política de Desenvolvimento dos Recursos Florestais e de Uso Racional das Terras na Amazônia* ("Basic Studies for the Establishment of a Policy for the Development of the Forestry Resources and the Rational Use of Lands in the Amazon"). According to this study, the reduced INCRA colonization program would be replaced by a new program for the commercial exploitation of timber resources in the Amazon Basin.

As part of this new program, SUDAM called for the establishment of twelve regional forests of production in the Amazon to promote rational methods of timber extraction and the industrial processing of woods. This new program would draw heavily upon the accumulated experience of several large international timber companies that were already in the Amazon. In addition, it would attempt to introduce the most modern forms of "sustained-yield" timber management. By rationalizing the process of land use in the Amazon, SUDAM officials claimed, Brazil would be able to protect its endangered forest patrimony, while at the same time becoming a major exporter of precious timber, paper and pulp products, and woods.[3]

In the following pages, I shall assess the economic and ecological significance of the above events. More specifically, two arguments will be presented that question the utility of the Brazilian government's response to the ecological crisis in the Amazon and that have critical importance for future environmental conditions in the region. First, I shall demonstrate that the real predators of the Amazon in recent years have been the large cattle ranchers in central Brazil and not, as has been frequently claimed, the peasant colonists from the Northeast. And, second, I shall show how the new commercial timber plan for the Amazon contains a fatal "technological flaw," and how it could threaten the ecology of the Amazon Basin even more than those land-use methods that have been practiced in the region in the past. Before doing so, however, it is necessary to discuss briefly the nature of Amazon ecology and to indicate the important role man has played in transforming the delicate balance of nature in this region of the world.[4]

The role of man in the Amazon

Despite the great interest in the Amazon by natural scientists in the nineteenth century, the first real scientific understanding of the ecology of the region did not occur until World War II. At that time, a Brazilian scientist named Felisberto C. de Camargo and his coworkers at the Agronomy Institute of the North in Belém began a series of studies of the ecology and agricultural potential of the Amazon Basin. Camargo was the first scientist who systematically recognized and described the critical differences between the two major ecological zones of the Amazon, the so-called *várzea* or Amazon floodplain and the vastly more extensive *terra firme* of the central and lower Amazon Basin. He was also the first scientist to describe the relatively poor climatic and edaphic conditions of the Amazon and to highlight the region's limits for human settlement. As a result of the studies of the Agronomy Institute of the North, scientists came to recognize the extremely delicate nature of the Amazon rain forest and to question the region's potential for uncontrolled agricultural exploitation and large-scale economic growth.[5]

At present, most scientists agree with the view of the Amazon first espoused by Camargo and his collaborators. Betty J. Meggers of the Smithsonian Institution in Washington, for example, has termed the Amazon "a counterfeit paradise," an area whose "fantastic complexity, infinite diversity, and marvelous integration" obscure what is essentially a "castle built on sand." The soil properties of the Amazon, Meggers writes, contribute:

nothing to the strength of the structure, and if enough components are removed or the bonds between them are sufficiently weakened, the entire configuration will collapse and disappear.

Meggers continues:

This is not merely a theoretical judgment based on soil composition, rainfall, temperature, chemical and physical properites, and other constituent factors; it is a conclusion increasingly supported by observation of the effects of modern human exploitation.[6]

A similar position has been expressed by Harald Sioli, director of the Max Planck Institute of Limnology in West Germany, who, like Meggers, has spent several years doing scientific research in the Amazon. Sioli describes the Amazon as being, like all large ecosystems, a vast "tension field," a focus of interaction between the environment, with its internal laws, and living organisms, such as man, with their internal laws and needs. "The intensiveness of the interactions between organism and environment," Sioli writes, "can be of very different degrees, ranging from almost imperceptible modifications inflicted on one or both partners to a ruthless struggle that may end with a total breakdown and death of one of them, a consequence that will then affect the survivor." In the Amazon, Sioli claims, this "tension field," with its now predictable consequences for both organisms and environment, is more delicate than in any other natural area of the world.[7]

Perhaps the most important feature of the Amazon studied by Felisberto C. de Camargo and his collaborators, and extended upon in recent scientific research, is the vast ecological difference between the *várzea* floodplain and the more extensive *terra firme* parts of the basin. The *várzea* makes up only 2 percent of the land area of the Amazon, but is covered by a network of lakes, ponds, and channels, and is characterized by a rich profusion of aquatic plant and animal life.

In contrast to other areas of the Amazon, the *várzea* is of recent geologic origin, dating back only to the end of the glacial period, when the rise in the ocean level drowned the wide river valleys of the lower Amazon, and when these rivers began to fill with the rich alluvium deposits from the headwater zones. Over the centuries, the Amazon River built up a relatively rich sediment base, derived directly or indirectly from the rivers of the High Andes, with their complex lithology and abundant volcanic materials. As a result of this geologic history, the soils of the *várzea* are less leached than those in other parts of the Amazon Basin and contain a large reserve of plant nutrients. In addition, every year, when the rains come and the Amazon River floods, a rich new layer of sediment is deposited along the stretches of the *várzea* plain.[8]

According to Camargo and his coworkers, the soil properties of the *várzea* provided ideal conditions for agriculture and human settlement. Camargo demonstrated that with a knowledge of the ecology of this zone and a system of agriculture geared to this ecology, a relatively large human population could subsist on the *várzea* without causing serious damage to the environment.

A more critical challenge, however, was posed by the much more extensive and soil-poor *terra firme* zone. The *terra firme* makes up more than 98 percent of the land area of the Amazon Basin. The soils of this region were laid down during the ancient Pliocene-Pleistocene period and were derived principally from the Guyana Shield to the north and the Central Brazilian Upland to the south. In some regions, these soils are up to 300 meters thick. They are composed of granitic and gneissic rocks and some sandstone, and they are poor in inorganic nutrients and plant growth. Most important, the warm temperatures and heavy rainfalls of the Amazon have intensely leached the soil substratum of the *terra firme*, making its composition extremely poor and acidic in quality. Meggers writes of the soils of the *terra firme* zone:

Millions of years of exposure to chemical weathering have leached out all soluble minerals, and the resulting "mature" soils consequently consist principally of sand and clay and are moderately to extremely acid. In terms of plant nutrients, the deficiencies are so severe that soils of a similar composition would be barren in a temperate climate.[9]

In recent decades, scientists have unraveled the puzzle of how the *terra firme* environment has maintained such a luxuriant plant cover on a base of such extremely poor and infertile soils. The key factor in the natural richness of the Amazon lies in the forest cover rather than the soil base. In essence, the tropical rain forest is a huge continuous canopy of evergreen foliage that fights off the detrimental effects of poor climatic and edaphic conditions, and serves the multiple functions of nutrient capture, nutrient storage, and the protection of soil from erosion and solar radiation.[10]

One way in which the forest performs these functions is by rechanneling nutrients to the poor soil base. Huge amounts of litter fall from the immense trees of the Amazon rain forest at a rate that is estimated to be three to four times greater than that of the New York woodlands. This litter contains double the amount of phosphorus and over ten times the amount of nitrogen found in temperate-climate forests.

The rainwater dripping from trees in the Amazon alone accounts for nearly 75 percent of the potassium, 40 percent of the magnesium, and 25 percent of the phosphorus available to plants at the base of the forest. Maximum utilization of these nutrients is insured by the wide diversity of plants, having different nutrient requirements and composed of a low concentration of individuals of the same species, which inhabit the forest floor. In turn, the poor soil is fortified when parts of this rich plant cover die and then return to the soil as inorganic matter for the processing of humus.

Another function of the forest is to serve as a protective cover against the powerful tropical rains. Studies reported by Meggers estimate that on the average 25 percent of the daily rainfall in the Amazon is withheld by the leaves of the large forest trees, and that the remainder reaches the ground in the form of a fine warm spray. An average annual rainfall of 85 inches on a forested slope of 12 to 15 percent in the Amazon, for example, is estimated to remove less than a ton of soil per acre over a three-year period. On the other hand, this same amount of rainfall on a deforested slope half as steep would remove as much as 45 tons of soil over a shorter period of time. Without the forest cover, in other words, the entire *terra firme* would quickly become leached and be rapidly washed away.[11]

These findings explain the calamitous effects that modern human activities have had on the ecology of the Amazon region. Until recently, the major form of agriculture practiced in the Amazon was a primitive form of slash-and-burn cultivation based on the use of fire and stone or steel axes. Under low population densities, this form of land usage did little harm to the delicate rain forest ecosystem. The short length of cultivation periods, the dispersion of clearings throughout the forest, the recycling of nutrients by fallen trees, branches, and weeds, and the intermixing of crops with different nutrient requirements all tended to maintain the balance of the ecosystem and to protect it against excessive erosion and destruction. After thirty to forty years of regeneration, areas brought under cultivation in this manner could be distinguished from the virgin forest only by a trained botanist. More intensive systems of cultivation under higher population densities, however, have tended to upset the natural ecology of the Amazon, and it is essentially these systems that have been most severely criticized by scientists in recent years.[12]

An excellent example of the effects of slash-and-burn agriculture under high population densities is provided by the colonization scheme developed in the Bragantina Zone east of Belém at the beginning of the present century. Between 1883 and 1908, a 300-kilometer railroad was constructed between Belém and the town of Bragança in order to stimulate settlement and to provide transportation for the farm and forest products of the region. Once the railroad was completed, the Brazilian government began to promote settler colonies in this region; over 1,000 colonists, mainly of Spanish, Portuguese, and French descent, immigrated to the Bragantina Zone. In 1915, this wave of migration increased when a drought struck the Northeast and when thousands of peasants were uprooted in the State of Ceará. By the late 1940s, the population density of Bragantina was one of the highest in the Amazon (eight inhabitants per square kilometer), and farmers had destroyed a forested area covering more than 30,000 square kilometers of land. [13]

Slash-and-burn agriculture under these high population densities proved devastating for the Bragantina Zone. During this period, farmers transformed the once-luxuriant forests of the Bragantina into what the Brazilian scientist Eugenia Gonçalves Egler has termed a "ghost landscape." Today, the Bragantina is covered by a monotonous expanse of unproductive secondary growth, lateritic sandstone, and rock. The soils in this region can no longer hold water, and droughts are much longer than they were in the past. With one of the largest populations in the State of Pará, the Bragantina is now considered to be a "semi-desert," a region whose lands have diminished yearly and whose soils have ceased to produce. [14]

Mary McNeil, an American scientist, describes a similar process of environmental destruction as having taken place at the President Dutra or Iata Colony along the Madeira and Madre de Dios rivers in the Brazilian territory of Rondônia. In the late 1940s, the Brazilian government sponsored an agricultural colonization experiment in this region to relocate destitute peasants who had been forced off the land in the Bragantina Zone of Pará. For the first three years, the crop yields at the Iata Colony were relatively good. In time, however, the soil was exhausted, and a process of laterization and erosion begun. "In less than five years," McNeil writes, "the cleared fields became virtually pavements of rock. Today, Iata is a drab, despairing colony that testifies eloquently to the formidable problems laterite presents throughout the tropics." [15]

In the Amazon Basin, McNeil claims, there are some accumulations of lateritic soil that are as much as 70 feet thick.

These are "truly fossil soils," which provide a record of the soil's several stages of evolution and which show the changes in climate, vegetation, topography, and geological processes that took place throughout the region's history. McNeil writes:

In the Brazilian profile we can see all the phases of the development of laterite, from its origin as a soil from the parent rock to its final transformation into the vast deposits of bauxite, manganese, iron, and new rock that now cover about 1,000 square miles of the Basin.[16]

The lessons of the Bragantina and Iata colonization experiments are clear. During the first half of the twentieth century, the role of man in the Amazon has been to speed up a process (soil laterization and erosion) that for centuries natural selection and evolution, by creating the rich plant and tree cover of the rain forest, have attempted to prevent. In almost every area of the Amazon where human occupation and agricultural settlement have been intense, this process of laterization has rapidly increased. Large-scale deforestation by human agents, in other words, has proved devastating for the delicate ecology of the Amazon and has destroyed vast expanses of once-productive tropical forests and lands.

The scope of deforestation activities in the Amazon

Since 1970, three socioeconomic-technological factors have speeded up the intensity of deforestation activities taking place in the Amazon Basin of Brazil. First, over the past few years, more men have been employed solely for purposes of land clearance in the Amazon than during any other period in Brazilian history. In 1971, for instance, a Brazilian journal reported that more than 6,000 men were working eight hours a day cutting down trees along the Trans-Amazon Highway. At the same time, another 50,000 men were employed in land-clearance operations associated with the SUDAM cattle-raising projects in central Brazil, and an additional 45,000 men were cutting commercial timber in the forests adjacent to the new roads. According to one estimate, over 300,000 hectares of virgin forest were cleared in the Amazon Basin in 1970 alone.[17]

Second, during this period, a wide array of new earthmoving machines was introduced in the Amazon Basin for purposes of highway construction, agriculture, and land clearance. As mentioned in Chapter 5, over the past few years a literal "tractor revolution" has been taking place in Brazil. In the Amazon and central Brazil, for example, cattle ranchers were purchasing large numbers of 90-and-over-horsepower tractors and crawlers for purposes of land clearance. In response to this demand, Ford was planning to reenter the Brazilian market with medium and heavy tractors. Massey-Ferguson was building a second plant and planning to introduce a 129-horsepower tractor. Caterpillar was building a new plant and planning to increase its production of D-4, D-7, and D-8 model tractors for use in agriculture. The introduction of these new machines marked a technological leap in man's capacity to transform the landscape of Brazil and had a major effect on the scope of land-clearance operations in the Amazon Basin.[18]

Finally, in recent years, cattle ranchers have begun to use chemical methods to clear lands and maintain pastures in the Amazon Basin. The actual scope of chemical herbicide use in Brazil is difficult to assess. In April 1973, however, the influential journal *Science* carried a report that noted that the U.S. Air Force was attempting to sell large quantities of Agent Orange, the chemical herbicide used to kill flora in Vietnam, to the Brazilian government and other governments in Latin America.

According to this article, the air force was attempting to find purchasers abroad for a stockpile of 2.3 million gallons of Agent Orange that it had stored at sites in the Pacific and along the Gulf Coast. Two private companies, Blue Spruce International and International Research, Inc., this article reported, were trying to arrange a contract for the sale of Agent Orange to the Brazilian government. Jerome F. Harrington, president of International

Research, was quoted by a *Science* reporter as saying that the Agent Orange could be diluted with gasoline and then sold to Brazilian ranchers for prices as low as $5 per gallon. By keeping rangelands cleared, Harrington claimed, such supplies of the chemical herbicide would increase Brazilian beef production by nearly $400 million per year and open up new markets in Latin America for U.S. agrochemical firms.[19]

In the weeks following the appearance of this article, environmentalists launched a successful campaign against the sale of Agent Orange to Brazil. Recent reports in the Brazilian press, however, indicate that chemical herbicides, such as 2,4-D and 2,4,5-T, outlawed for use on grazing lands in the United States, are actually being used by cattle ranchers in the Amazon region of Brazil. Alceo Magnanini, director of the Department of Research and Nature Conservation of the Brazilian Institute of Forestry Development (IBDF), is quoted as saying in a recent article that the usage of the herbicide 2,4,5-T in the Amazon "brings immediate, middle, and long range threats to the human species." The dioxin compound in this chemical, he claims, "contains poisonous, teratological, and possibly carcinogenic substances." To date, Magnanini says, all attempts to control its usage have been unsuccessful in Brazil.[20]

All the above factors explain the serious concern scientists and ecologists have shown for the future of the Amazon in recent years. In one of the early reports on the environmental impact of the Brazilian government's development program, for example, a German ecologist noted that he observed a single cattle company with a team of 1,000 men at work in the Amazon, cutting down the forest and indiscriminately ruining the land. If land clearance continued on this scale, this ecologist predicted, around 1990 there would be a "series of ecological crises" throughout the Amazon region of Brazil. There were compelling scientific reasons, he argued, for a reconsideration of the Brazilian government's programs and plans.[21]

Other experts within Brazil have echoed the warnings of this ecologist. For example, Roberto Burle Marx, one of Brazil's best-known landscape architects, has compared the present destruction taking place in the Amazon to what happened in the area along the Atlantic Coast, where colonists ruthlessly destroyed over 300 kilometers of virgin forest in the first years following the Portuguese discovery of Brazil. In comparison, Burle Marx wrote:

What is happening along the Trans-Amazon Highway is even more critical. Immense areas are being destroyed for pasturage and colonization schemes. These areas are being transformed into deserts, because there is no precise knowledge of what to plant and what is best for the soil.[22]

Similar warnings have been voiced by Marvick Kleer of the University of Riberão Preto in Brazil. Speaking before the Twenty-Sixth Annual Meeting of the Brazilian Society for the Progress of Science in 1974, Kleer predicted that within the next thirty years the entire Amazon rain forest would be destroyed if deforestation trends continued at their present rates. According to Kleer, in the past ten years more than 24 percent of the Amazon had been destroyed by the reckless felling of trees.[23]

Official statistics on the scope of recent deforestation activities in the Amazon Basin released by the Brazilian Institute of Forestry Development (IBDF) tend to substantiate these predictions and claims. Between 1960 and 1970, for example, population along the Belém–Brasília Highway increased from 1 million to 2 million. By this time, over 5 million head of cattle were being raised in this area of Brazil. A report issued by the IBDF indicated that certain cleared areas in this region were already "turning into deserts." The erosion caused by such activity, this report noted, was not only making the soil infertile in as short as three to four years, but was also reducing the runoff of rain into nearby rivers. "These sorts of agricultural and cattle raising activities," an official of the IBDF was quoted as saying, "are able to destroy the forest patrimony of the Amazon in the same way as the eco-

Table 3. *Area of land officially deforested in the Brazilian Amazon, 1966–1975 (in hectares)*

Type of project	Area deforested	Percent of total area
Cattle-raising		
With fiscal incentives (SUDAM)	3,865,271	33.6
Without fiscal incentives	510,000	4.4
Total	4,375,271	38.0
Colonization		
State-directed (INCRA)	2,019,480	17.6
Private	1,500,000	13.1
Total	3,519,480	30.7
Highways		
Belém–Brasília	1,100,000	9.6
Trans–Amazon	675,000	5.9
Others	1,300,000	11.3
Total	3,075,000	26.8
Forestry	500,000	4.4
Total area deforested	11,469,751	100.0

Source: Brazilian Institute of Forestry Development (IBDF), cited in O *Estado de São Paulo* (November 11, 1975), p. 60.

nomic cycles of sugar cane and coffee were responsible for the destruction of the Northeast and the South."[24]

More recently, the IBDF has released statistics on the amount of officially authorized deforestation that took place in the Amazon Basin between 1966 and 1975 (see Table 3). The interesting feature of this data is that the major elements responsible for the deforestation of the Brazilian Amazon have been the large-scale cattle-ranching projects promoted by SUDAM (3,865,271 hectares) and the highway construction program of the Brazilian government (3,075,000 hectares). Together, these two elements accounted for 60 percent of the land area deforested in the

Amazon. In contrast, the INCRA colonization program, in which peasant colonists from the Northeast were involved, accounted for only 17.6 percent of the land area that was destroyed.

Most important, the rate of deforestation attributable to these large-scale cattle-ranching projects has been increasing in recent years. In 1973, for example, 187,253 hectares of land were cleared for cattle-ranching projects in the south of Pará. A year later, in 1974, this figure more than doubled to 414,894 hectares. One source claims that the rhythm of deforestation activities in the Amazon has been increasing at a rate of 30 percent per year. Already, an area of land the size of the Brazilian Territory of Amapá has been destroyed.[25]

In 1971, Harald Sioli made public a series of rough calculations concerning the long-range meteorological impact of recent deforestation activities in the Brazilian Amazon. Sioli's calculations focused international attention on the important role that photosynthetic processes in the Amazon played in determining the amount of carbon dioxide and oxygen in the earth's atmosphere. Attempting to predict the potential atmospheric effects of burning the entire rain forest, Sioli calculated that the Amazon Basin contains approximately 600 tons of organic matter per hectare of land and holds about 300 tons of carbon per hectare. Multiplying these figures by the total area of the rain forest, he estimated that, through the process of plant photosynthesis, the Amazon Basin produces roughly 50 percent of the oxygen added to the earth's atmosphere annually, and consumes about 10 percent of the gaseous carbon available in the atmosphere. The burning of the Amazon rain forest, Sioli warned, would send vast quantities of stored carbon (perhaps as high as 70 percent of that already existent in the atmosphere) into the air, and have unpredictable but drastic effects on the earth's temperature.[26]

Sioli's calculations about the role that the Amazon rain forest plays in the supply of oxygen and carbon dioxide in the earth's atmosphere were not meant to be exact predictions. He raised these issues merely to focus attention on the potential "ecological backlashes" that might be caused by the deforestation of the Brazilian Amazon. According to Sioli, the Amazon Basin covers more than a million square miles and contains about one-third of the trees on the earth's surface. Leveling this region with fire, tractors, or chemical herbicides would be like getting rid of one of the world's major oceans. It would have disastrous effects on the entire biosphere and upset the delicately balanced conditions of the earth. From a planetary point of view, Sioli claimed, the continuance of present deforestation trends in the Amazon could only be environmentally suicidal in its effects. [27]

Environmental effects of the Polamazônia Program

In 1974, a number of critics, both within and outside the government, called for a "new model" for the ecologically sound occupation and settlement of the Brazilian Amazon. At the time these criticisms were being voiced, the Superintendency for the Development of the Amazon (SUDAM) was already setting the groundwork for the full-scale rationalization of all land-use patterns in the Amazon. In the months previous to the announcement of the new *Polamazônia* Program, for example, SUDAM released a detailed report which noted that the original Plan for National Integration (PIN) did not include a program for the exploitation of the vast timber resources of the Amazon Basin. According to this report, the Amazon Basin contained over 45 billion (American billion) metric feet of commercial timber. Forestry experts expected the timber reserves of Africa to be exhausted within thirteen to thirty years and those of South Asia within twenty-seven to thirty years. By 1985, the SUDAM report asserted, the Brazilian Amazon could dominate the international market in timber, paper and pulp products, and tropical woods. [28]

Specifically, the SUDAM report suggested that three major programs be implemented in the Amazon Basin. First, it called for the technological modernization of all lumbering operations in the region. According to SUDAM, most timber operations in the Amazon were still of an empirical or primitive sort and had not yet introduced the modern methods of timber extraction used by companies in countries such as Canada and the United States. In order to alleviate this situation, SUDAM called for a major government program that would introduce modern methods of timber extraction, improve river and terrestrial transportation, and provide for the creation of a fleet of "floating sawmills" in the Amazon Basin. This program of technological innovation, the SUDAM report claimed, would transform the economic backwardness of the timber industry in the Amazon and decrease the amount of environmental depredation and waste.[29]

Second, SUDAM called for the further promotion of industrial wood-processing activities in the Amazon Basin. Since the late 1960s, the SUDAM report noted, the industrial processing of forest materials had grown significantly in the region. Three large international companies – the Georgia Pacific Corporation of the United States, the Bruynzeel Company of Holland, and the Toyomenka Corporation of Japan – had already established large veneer factories and tree plantations at strategic locations near the mouth of the Amazon River. In addition, six other large lumber corporations were elaborating plans to locate in the Amazon.

The SUDAM report claimed that it was important that all timber-extraction activities in the Amazon be geared to the supply needs of these industrial firms. Further, it suggested that other "integrated industrial complexes" should be set up in the Amazon on the model of the huge tree-farming experiment that Daniel Keith Ludwig had created on his Jari Forestry and Ranching Estate.[30]

Finally, the SUDAM report called for the establishment of twelve regional forests of production in the Amazon covering over 50 million hectares of land. According to SUDAM, the new aerial-photographic surveys provided by Project Radam now made it possible to plan "macro-regional" land-use areas in the Amazon Basin. Using these surveys, SUDAM had mapped out twelve areas in the Basin for the creation of several "sustained-

Table 4. *Projected land-use patterns in the Brazilian Amazon (in millions of hectares)*

Type of land use	Estimated area	Percent of total area
Areas cleared for nonforestry purposes	78.8	30.3
Areas cleared for agricultural purposes	40.0	15.4
Natural pasturage	15.0	5.8
Floodplains, swamps, and mangroves	9.5	3.7
Indian reserves	20.0	7.7
National parks and biological reserves	43.0	16.5
"Sustained-yield" forest reserves	53.7	20.7
Total area	260.0	100.0

Source: Serete S.A., cited in Brazilian Ministry of the Interior, Superintendency for the Development of the Amazon (SUDAM), Department of Natural Resources, *Estudos Básicos Para O Estabelecimento de Uma Política de Desenvolvimento Dos Recursos Florestais e De Uso Racional das Terras na Amazônia* (Belém, 1974), p. 51.

yield" forest reserves. These areas were to serve a different function than national parks and biological reserves and were to form the basis for the government's new commercial forestry plan. Specifically, the SUDAM report suggested that the government place these areas under public ownership and create a special mixed, part private and part state-owned, company for the exploitation and management of these reserves.[31]

Table 4 shows the projected future land-use patterns in the Amazon Basin as envisioned in the new forestry plan of SUDAM. As can be seen from this table, SUDAM expects at least 53.7 million hectares of land, or about one-fifth of the area of the Amazon Basin, to be eventually composed of "sustained-yield" forest reserves. The basic idea behind this program is that areas of the Amazon can be cleared for commercial timbers and then replanted to reproduce the original forest cover. This idea is based on forest-utilization and management practices developed in Canada and the United States. In simplest terms, it assumes that the Amazon rain forest is a renewable resource, which through temperate-climate methods of land management can be replanted and produce "sustained-yield" forestry harvests. On both historical and scientific grounds, there are reasons to believe that this assumption is environmentally dangerous, foolhardy, and untrue.[32]

Aside from Daniel Keith Ludwig's recent venture in the Territory of Amapá, the only major large-scale tree-farming experiment in the Amazon Basin to date has been Henry Ford's unsuccessful Fordlândia and Belterra rubber plantations in the State of Pará. In 1926, the Brazilian government granted Ford a large 10,000-square-kilometer land concession along the Tapajós River to create the first modern rubber plantation in South America. Ford's purposes in creating Fordlândia were to prove that temperate-climate tree-farming methods could be profitably and successfully applied in the Amazon Basin. In time, Ford hoped that his Amazon tree-farming experiment would be as profitable as similar rubber plantation ventures carried out by French and British entrepreneurs in Indochina and South Asia.

Originally, workers on the Fordlândia estate planted 800,000 rubber trees. From the beginning, however, several problems plagued the Fordlândia plantation. The most critical of these problems was the presence of a disease in the Amazon, the "South American leaf disease" (*dothidella ulei*), which was unknown in South Asia. In 1932, this disease attacked the new secondary forest cover of the Fordlândia plantation. The disease caused severe damage and destroyed almost all the newly planted trees on the Ford estate.

After several unsuccessful attempts at eradicating this disease, in 1934 Ford exchanged one-quarter of his Fordlândia estate for another area of land located about 100 kilometers down the Tapajós River. At this site, Ford established a new plantation called Belterra and planted nearly 2 million rubber trees. Again, though, the leaf disease struck, and in 1936 agronomists on the

Ford estate were forced to introduce an expensive and time-consuming method of double grafting to save the remaining trees on the Belterra estate.

Following World War II, Henry Ford handed over his two plantations to the Brazilian government, which, in turn assigned them to the Agronomy Institute of the North in Belém. For a period of years, Felisberto C. de Camargo and his collaborators experimented with various forms of rational timber management and reforestation on these estates. Some of these experiments were successful, but they were extremely costly and, from an economic point of view, infeasible. More recently, these experiments have also been abandoned. In their place, the Agronomy Institute of the North has attempted smaller experiments that are based on the natural ecology of the Amazon region and apply modern methods of landscape ecological thinking.[33]

In 1972, three Mexican botanists, A. Gómez-Pompa, C. Vásquez-Yanes, and S. Guevara, published an article in *Science* that described some of the reasons why tropical rain forests were incapable of regeneration under present land-use practices. Although the scientific evidence was still incomplete, these scientists argued that there were compelling reasons for believing that the processes of primary-forest regeneration were much more complex and delicate in tropical rain forest ecosystems than in temperate-climate forests.

Under aboriginal systems of shifting cultivation, these scientists noted, the delicate system of rain forest regeneration is seldom upset and is more or less able to respond in the same way as when localized natural catastrophes, such as heavy storms, strike the primary forest. However, more intensive systems of land use, such as those associated with modern agricultural and forestry techniques, ruin this delicate system of forest regeneration. Under these systems of land use, the seeds of primary-tree species, because of their dispersal characteristics and their scarcity, become less and less available. In turn, those seeds that are available are of secondary species, which are preadapted to continuous disturbances, or of new species brought in from drier environments. These species have characteristics that enable them to thrive under conditions of massive disturbance. Unlike the primary-forest species, they tend to produce large quantities of seeds and have a longer life span in the soil. The process often called "savannization" or "desertization" in the tropics can be explained by these facts.

According to Gómez-Pompa, Vásquez-Yanes, and Guevara, the implications of these facts were clear. Throughout the tropics, there is a great danger that thousands of species of primary-forest trees will become extinct. The reason for this process of mass destruction is that tropical rain forest tree species are incapable of recolonizing large areas under conditions of intensive or extensive land use. Because of the specific nature of their successional patterns, these rain forest tree species behave in a radically different way from tree species in temperate-climate environments. "All the evidence available," these scientists concluded, "supports the idea that, under present intensive use of the land in tropical rainforest regions, the ecosystems are in danger of a mass extinction of most of their species."[34]

The historical and scientific evidence cited above provides reasons for believing that the entire notion of "sustained-yield" forest management, as used in the SUDAM report of 1974, is a contradiction in terms in the tropics. This notion contains a serious "technological flaw." Namely, it assumes that commercial timber-clearing practices and technologies developed in temperate-climate countries such as Canada and the United States can be transferred with only slight modifications to the Amazon Basin without causing irreparable damage to the tropical rain forest ecosystem. The usage of these technologies raises severe environmental issues within temperate-climate countries themselves. To transfer them to the Amazon Basin appears economically shortsighted and environmentally insane.[35]

In recent years, several ecologically minded scientists have made a strong case for the usage of indigenous, rather than imported, models for the development of the Amazon. In a symposium on the future of the threatened Cintas Largas Indian tribe held in Cuiabá, Mato Grosso, in 1973, for example, Paulo de Almeida Machado, director of Brazil's National Institute for Amazon Research, compared what was taking place in the Amazon to a race between science and development. Machado explained how the Amazon rain forest, which is roughly the same size as the United States, was a unique ecological system and noted how little was presently known about the ways it functions. Trying to transfer knowledge and technology developed in other parts of the world to the Amazon, Machado claimed, could only lead to economic and ecological disaster. "If we violate this system," he said, "we cannot replace it by planting other trees, such as bananas. We will have to study it in depth and use imagination and immense creativity to find new forms of agriculture that fit in with this reality."

In the course of his speech, Machado suggested that perhaps the only solution to the problem of the Amazon was possessed by the surviving Indian tribes who have inhabited the region for thousands of years. "We regard the Indian," Machado stated, "as an inferior being with an inferior culture. But when you talk about living in the Amazon he is far superior because he harmonizes so perfectly with the whole ecological system."

Machado went on to argue that Western man prides himself on his ability to dominate nature, and hence has failed to comprehend the many ways in which Indians have learned to harmonize with nature, while at the same time using it for their needs. The Indian, he said, has hundreds of crops that are not used by Western man, do not upset the ecological system, and could be exploited commercially. The Indian also possesses vast stores of cultural knowledge about medicines and other remedies, and in his natural condition is free from malaria and other Western diseases. Finally, the Indian has learned to balance population with resources, and for centuries has lived in the Amazon without poisoning its waters and lands. "The tragedy," Machado concluded, "is that the Indian is one of the main keys to the successful occupation of the Amazon, and as he disappears his vast wealth of knowledge is going with him."[36]

10

The Amazon Basin: implications for U.S. foreign policy in Brazil

We are in disagreement with the repeated statements of the Minister of the Interior that "The Indian problem is a problem for Brazil," and that "other countries know nothing about the problem of the Brazilian Indian." The misnamed "Indian Problem" is a problem for humanity, a problem whose causes and motivations are perhaps better known in countries where there is freedom of information and discussion than in Brazil.

In the final analysis, there are millions of human beings in the Americas and several thousands in Brazil, who, for centuries, have suffered the gravest injustices inflicted by a "race" which claims to be superior. If the conscience of humanity were equal to the volume of information, such an iniquitous situation would no longer be tolerated. The "Indian Problem" in Brazil cannot be understood, and much less solved, unless it is situated in its international context.

from Y-Juca-Pirama, an urgent document released by the bishops and priests of the Brazilian Amazon on the twenty-fifth anniversary of the Universal Declaration of Human Rights, December 25, 1973

In his well-known essay of 1957, "Indigenous Cultures and Languages of Brazil," Darcy Ribeiro argued that Brazilian national society presented a series of "diverse faces" to Indians (what he called the "faces of civilization") depending upon whether it took the shape of an extractive, pastoral, or agricultural economy. According to Ribeiro, each of these different types of economic frontiers was motivated by unlike interests in its exploitation of the environment, each was organized in terms of its own structural principles, and each imposed its own distinctive constraints on the tribal groups it confronted. The extractive frontier, Ribeiro claimed, was made up of individuals, who were detached from their communities of origin and who moved into unexplored territories inhabited by isolated or hostile tribal groups. The pastoral frontier was usually composed of family groups, who advanced into unexplored areas in search of new pastures for their herds and who dispossessed Indians of their lands. Finally, the expanding agricultural frontier generally involved larger human populations, who rapidly and drastically transformed the landscape and who saw Indians as an obstacle in their path. In reference to this last type of frontier, Ribeiro wrote:

Agricultural pioneers see the Indian as merely an obstacle to their expansion, and they resort to conflict to take possession of the lands he occupies and thus extend the area in use for agricultural production. . . . Within a few years, the Indians find themselves obliged to adopt new forms of eking out subsistence and surrounded by a relatively dense population to whose ways of life they must accommodate if they are to survive.[1]

In the pages of this book, I have analyzed several of the new structural factors that have been at work in transforming the nature of frontier expansion, and hence interethnic conflicts, in the Amazon Basin of Brazil. Basically, I have argued that three new factors have transformed the nature of Brazilian frontier phenomena since the military coup of 1964 and the announcement of the Trans-Amazon Highway in 1970. The first of these factors has been the strategic role that the Brazilian government has played in the opening up and settlement of the Amazon Basin. The second factor has been the dominant economic role that large multinational and state-owned business corporations have assumed in the exploitation of the rich mineral, timber, and agricultural resources of the region. The third factor has been the increasing importance that loans from international lending institutions and foreign banks have played in the financing of infrastructural projects in the Amazon.

In essence, the nature of economic expansion in Brazil today is something different from what it was when Darcy Ribeiro carried out his studies of interethnic conflict in the decades of the 1950s and 1960s. Over the past decade, a new partnership has emerged in Brazil between a highly repressive, but development-conscious, military government, a number of multinational and state-owned firms, and several international lending institutions such as the Export-Import Bank, the Inter-American Development Bank, and the World Bank. This new partnership, which is hardly unique to Brazil, has speeded up the pace of economic expansion into the last refuge areas inhabited by Indian tribes and has begun to replace the several diverse, but relatively backward, economic frontiers that Darcy Ribeiro first analyzed in his essay of 1957. Further, the evidence contained in this book indicates that three important consequences have resulted from this new partnership in the Amazon Basin of Brazil.[2]

First, since 1970, the Brazilian National Indian Foundation (FUNAI) has institutionalized a new type of Indian policy that is consistent with the larger economic development objectives of the Brazilian military regime, but which has proven devastating for Brazilian Indian tribes. As an agency within the Brazilian Ministry of the Interior, the main objectives of FUNAI policy have been twofold: first, to integrate Indian tribes as rapidly as possible into Brazilian national society; and, second, to insure that these tribes do not serve as an obstacle in the way of national progress and economic growth. Perhaps the major area where these objectives are reflected is in the new Brazilian Indian Statute. This statute, which became law in December 1973, provides FUNAI with the right to relocate Indians out of their traditional tribal territories for reasons of national security and development. In addition, it enables the official government agency, under what is called the "indigenous income," to lease Indian mineral, timber, and agricultural reserves.

In several cases, it has been shown how FUNAI was forced to sacrifice Indian land rights for the larger economic interests of state highway programs, large-scale mining projects, and agribusiness enterprises in the Amazon. Such wanton dispossession of native lands has led to the uprooting and destruction of scores of Indian tribes. Without a major change in policy, one can only predict that a similar fate awaits other Indian tribes in Brazil. This is particularly true in the far northern part of the Amazon Basin, where highway and mining development projects presently threaten the territorial integrity of the large Yanomamö and Waimirí-Atroarí tribes.[3]

Second, recent economic changes in the Amazon region have tended to worsen rather than alleviate the severe agrarian problems of Brazil. In Chapter 8 of this book, for example, it was demonstrated how recent economic transformations in the Amazon Basin have affected the large rural and peasant populations of the region. Over the past decade, large-scale cattle ranching has replaced peasant small-holding as the basic pattern of land occupation in Mato Grosso and central Brazil. The introduction of these new ranches has had the full support of the military government and has received significant financial inputs from industrial capitalists and agribusinessmen in the South of Brazil. Among the foreign companies now involved in agribusiness enterprises in the Amazon are the King Ranch of Texas, Daniel Keith Ludwig of National Bulk Carriers, the Liquigas firm of Italy, and the German automobile manufacturer, Volkswagen.[4]

One of the major results of this new settlement pattern has been the uprooting of large numbers of poor Brazilian peasants who previously formed the pioneer element in central Brazil. It must be stated categorically that the land-tenure situation of these peasant small-holders is no less precarious than that of Indian groups in the Amazon Basin. In addition, all attempts to seek legal protection for the land claims of these peasant populations, on the part of such institutions as the Brazilian Catholic church, have been met by severe repression on the part of local, state, and national officials in Brazil. As a result, over the past decade, agrarian protest and violence have reached epidemic proportions in several areas of Mato Grosso and central Brazil.[5]

At the same time as these changes have been taking place in the Amazon, agrarian problems have also worsened in the far more populous northeastern region of Brazil. According to SU-DENE, the Superintendency for the Development of the Northeast, at present more than 5 million people are either jobless or underemployed in the Northeast of Brazil. On the national level, the average annual income is approximately $750. In the Northeast, this figure drops to about $150. More than half the population of the Northeast over fifteen years of age is illiterate. Because of epidemics and malnutrition in this area, the population of the Northeast has one of the lowest life expectancy rates in Latin America. In the worst rural zones, health authorities estimate that infant mortality rates are as high as 25 percent.[6]

A recent *New York Times* article notes that the continuing economic backwardness of the Northeast has created "widespread pessimism" about the efficacy of the "economic development model" adopted by the Brazilian military regime. There is no doubt, this article states, that this model has created a "spectacular economic surge" during the last seven years. Most of this growth, however, has been confined to the central and southern parts of Brazil. "The Northeast, if anything," this article states, "has grown relatively poorer."[7]

Finally, recent economic changes in Brazil have caused havoc in the delicate ecology of the Amazon rain forest. The reasons for this widespread ecological destruction are *not* to be found in a lack of concern for the environment on the part of the Brazilian people relative to other peoples or nations of the world. To the contrary, the causes for the rapacious destruction of the Amazon rain forest are to be found in the same set of factors that are uprooting Indian and peasant populations in Brazil. Namely, over the past several years, the Brazilian government has been extremely successful in obtaining a wide array of modern technology for purposes of land clearance and deforestation in the Amazon Basin. Among these technologies are several new types of tractors used for building highways through the jungle, chemical herbicides that are dropped from low-flying airplanes for purposes of maintaining grasslands, and various clear-cutting technologies made available in the Amazon through the presence of international timber, paper, and pulp firms.

The environmental rationality of these new land-clearance technologies is somewhat questionable even in the temperate-climate countries where they have been produced. In the case of Brazil, however, the usage of these technologies has proven economically profitable, and hence there has been little desire on the part of the military government to assess their ecological impact or to set standards of environmental control. Robert J. A. Goodland, a staff ecologist at the Cary Arboretum of the New York Botanical Garden, sums up the issues involved in the ecological destruction of the Amazon in the following terms:

At stake in the Amazon is the future of an area of one-half million square miles, larger than all of Europe and containing one-third of the world's remaining forest land. . . . Under Brazil's present development policies, it is being obliterated. The derisory short-term gains that the developers are seeking surely will be supplanted by desperate long-term problems, unless remedial action is undertaken soon.[8]

Unfortunately, most American foreign policy makers have tended to overlook these social and environmental consequences of the Brazilian model of development and have tended to provide official support for U.S. corporations with large investments in Brazil. In May 1976, for example, William Simon, then secretary of the treasury of the United States, held a series of important meetings with the Brazilian minister of finance, Mario Henrique Simonsen. Ostensibly, these meetings were to work out a number of trade agreements under which Brazil would remove export incentives on such items as shoes, leather goods, and soya oil. In the course of these meetings, however, several other important items were also discussed. One of these was the need for greater investment on the part of U.S. corporations in Brazil. According to one report, the Brazilian minister of planning, João Reis Velloso, presented Treasury Secretary Simon with a list of private investment opportunities totaling over $77,200 million in the next five years. Among the items on this list were new mining, pulp, board, and oil projects, and a large number of previously unannounced hydroelectric plants in the Amazon Basin.

During these meetings, Secretary Simon was reported to have indicated that the Brazilian planning minister's scheme for increased foreign investment would be viable if Brazil could provide U.S. corporations with further assurances and securities on their capital. Secretary Simon referred particularly to the highly controversial "law of profit remittances," which was then under discussion in Brazil. This law was first passed in 1962, and later amended following the military coup of 1964. It allows foreign corporations doing business in Brazil to have tax-free remittances of 12 percent of invested and reinvested capital and, to compensate for poor performance in any one year, to calculate their capital gains over a three-year period at 36 percent. Once this limit is reached, a progressive tax is applied to foreign capital gains in Brazil. "Simon," a *Latin America Economic Report* article noted, "said he would encourage United States corporations to invest in Brazil, but warned that ways would have to be found of eliminating double taxation liability."[9]

While then–Secretary of the Treasury Simon's position reflects official American foreign policy in Brazil, other public officeholders in this country have expressed a more critical view of U.S. government policy abroad. The views of some of these officeholders have direct relevance for several of the issues raised in this book.

In May 1971, for example, the U.S. Senate Subcommittee on Western Hemisphere Affairs held a series of hearings on the subject of U.S. policies and programs in Brazil. In opening these hearings, Senator Frank Church of Idaho noted that:

How Brazilians organize their own affairs and how they treat each other are no proper concern of the U.S. Senate. How the various agencies of the U.S. Government conduct themselves in Brazil, and how they react to events there, are proper concerns of all Americans.

Specific attention during these hearings focused upon the position of U.S. agencies in relation to questions of political repression and torture in Brazil. In the course of these hearings, however, some members of the Senate subcommittee also showed an interest in the Brazilian economy and in Brazil's program to open up and exploit the Amazon region.[10]

Since 1971, two further congressional actions have been taken that could potentially bear on the issues raised in this book. The first of these was the establishment within the Senate Foreign Relations Committee of a special Subcommittee on Multinational Corporations. This subcommittee held its first hearings in March 1973. In introducing these hearings, it was revealed that the U.S. Congress was about to conduct a "broad examination of the role of multinational corporations, their influence on U.S. foreign policy, and their economic impact." Among the many questions the new subcommittee would attempt to answer was the "extent to which there is a coincidence of interest between the multinational corporations and U.S. foreign policy in selected areas of the world." As noted in Chapter 3 of this book, in August 1975 Richard S. Newfarmer and Willard F. Mueller of the University of Wisconsin submitted a report to the subcommittee titled, *Multinational Corporations in Brazil and Mexico: Structural Sources of Economic and Noneconomic Power.*[11]

A second major action taken by the U.S. Congress was the holding of a series of hearings on the subject of the international protection of human rights. These hearings were conducted by the House Subcommittee on International Organizations and Movements in August through December of 1973. A report issued by eight of the eleven members of the subcommittee asserted that the prevailing attitude of U.S. foreign policy was to favor power politics at the expense of human rights. In relations with such countries as South Vietnam, Spain, Portugal, the Soviet Union, Brazil, Indonesia, Greece, the Philippines, and Chile, the subcommittee report charged, the United States "had disregarded human rights for the sake of other assumed interests," and "embraced governments who practice torture and unabashedly violate almost every human rights guarantee pronounced by the world community." In its recommendations, members of this subcommittee urged the United States to act on its own or in United Nations forums to try to prevent other governments from practicing torture and massacre, and called upon the administration to "treat human rights factors as a regular part of United States foreign policy decision-making."[12]

Since the military coup in Chile in 1973, a number of members of Congress have taken a more active position on the question of human rights violations in Latin America. In 1975, for example, human rights advocates in Congress introduced an amendment to U.S. aid legislation (the so-called Harkin Amendment) that specifically forbids giving U.S. assistance to the "government of any country which engages in a consistent pattern of gross violations of internationally recognized human rights." Recently, this amendment has been used to block military assistance to the governments of Uruguay and Chile. Discussions have also taken place in Congress on blocking military and economic assistance to the governments of Brazil, Argentina, and Paraguay.[13]

One of the major conclusions of this book is that there is a need for a broader definition of the concept of "human rights" as it applies to American foreign policy and to the provisioning of military assistance and economic aid. To date, most concern for these matters in Congress has only focused on gross violations of political and legal rights. Any reasonable and humane reformulation of American foreign policy, however, should go far beyond such a limited definition of "human rights." It should include, for example, some minimal definition of the rights of ethnic minorities, and it should provide some mechanism to insure that

United States aid does not threaten these rights. Likewise, it should recognize those aspects of "human rights" that usually fall under the broad category of "economic justice." In this regard, it should establish guidelines to insure that American aid programs reach those people who are truly poor, hungry, and in need of aid. Finally, a reformulated American foreign policy should set specific standards for the practices of U.S. multinational corporations abroad. At the least, it should establish legal mechanisms to insure that these multinational corporations do not carry out activities in other countries that would be deemed unlawful at home.

Over the past decade, a number of nongovernmental organizations have been created to bring international opinion to bear on the serious threat posed to the survival of indigenous populations throughout the world. Among these organizations are the International Work Group for Indigenous Affairs in Denmark, Amazind in Switzerland, Survival International in England, and INDIGENA and Cultural Survival in the United States. To date, however, the issues raised by these organizations have hardly penetrated world opinion and have only received slight notice in the international press. I have written this book in the hope that international attention will now focus on the issues raised by these organizations. One of the ways in which this might be done, I believe, is through a greater concern on the part of recognized international agencies and national governments with the devastating impact that recent economic development programs are having on indigenous populations, peasants, rural workers, and the earth.[14]

At the present moment, a silent war is being waged against aboriginal peoples, innocent peasants, and the rain forest ecosystem in the Amazon Basin of South America. To many readers, it may appear as if the immense suffering and damage caused in the Amazon Basin is one of the inevitable costs that must be assumed by any country that wishes to experience rapid economic growth. This position, I believe, is a mistaken one. There is nothing inevitable about what is taking place in the Brazilian Amazon. Nor are there any compelling reasons for believing that the Amazon development program will benefit the vast majority of the people of Brazil. The silent war being waged against the people and environment of the Amazon Basin is the result of a very specific "model of development." Today, this "model of development" is being implemented in several other frontier areas of the world. A counter wave of public sentiment, which questioned the priorities of international development policy, and which held foreign policy makers, international lending institutions, and multinational corporations accountable for their activities in these frontier areas, would be a major step in bringing this and other similar wars to a halt.

Notes

Preface and acknowledgments

1 For a discussion of the life and works of Noel Nutels, see the essay by Darcy Ribeiro, "Pensando em Noel," in Noel Nutels, *Memórias e Depoimentos* (Rio de Janeiro, 1974), pp. 87–93.

2 An overview of the methodology and perspective of the North American Congress on Latin America can be found in two publications of this organization: NACLA *Research Methodology Guide* (New York, 1970), and *Yanqui Dollar: The Contribution of U.S. Private Investment to Underdevelopment in Latin America* (New York, 1971).

3 Joseph G. Jorgensen, "Indians and the Metropolis," in J. O. Waddell and O. M. Watson (eds.), *The American Indian in Urban Society* (Boston, 1971), pp. 67–113; and, *The Sun Dance Religion: Power for the Powerless* (Chicago, 1972). Also, Andre Gunder Frank, *Capitalism and Underdevelopment in Latin America* (New York, 1967).

4 Laura Nader, "Up the Anthropologist – Perspectives Gained From Studying Up," in Dell Hymes (ed.), *Reinventing Anthropology* (New York, 1969), pp. 284–311.

5 Gerald D. Berreman, "Is Anthropology Alive? Social Responsibility in Social Anthropology," *Current Anthropology*, 9, No. 5 (1968), pp. 391–6; and " 'Bringing It All Back Home': Malaise in Anthropology," in Dell Hymes (ed.), *Reinventing Anthropology*, pp. 83–98.

6 At the time of the November 1974 press conference, INDIGENA and American Friends of Brazil published a short pamphlet titled, *Supysáua: A Documentary Report on the Conditions of Indian Peoples in Brazil* (Berkeley, Calif., 1974).

1. Brazilian Indian policy: an historical overview

1 Darcy Ribeiro, *Os Indios e a Civilização: A Integração Das Populações Indígenas no Brasil Moderno* (Rio de Janeiro, 1970), Chapter 3.

2 See the articles by Hermann von Ihering, director of the Museu Paulista: "A Antropologia do Estado de São Paulo," *Revista do Museu Paulista*, 7 (1907), 202–57; and "A Questão dos Indios no Brasil," *Revista do Museu Paulista*, 8 (1911), 112–40.

3 David Stauffer, "Origem e Fundação do Serviço de Proteção aos Indios (1889/1910)," *Revista de História* (São Paulo, 1959 and 1960), 73–95, 435–53.

4 Vincenzo Petrullo, "General Cândido Mariano da Silva Rondon: Sertanista and Indianist," *America Indígena*, 2, No. 1 (Mexico, 1942), 80–3.

5 Darcy Ribeiro, "A Obra Indigenista de Rondon," *America Indígena*, 19, No. 2 (1959), 85–113.

6 Darcy Ribeiro, *A Política Indigenista Brasileira* (Rio de Janeiro, 1962).

7 Darcy Ribeiro, "Brazil's Indian Frontier," *Americas*, 6, No. 3 (Washington, D.C., 1954), 18.

8 Ribeiro's study originally appeared under the title, "Culturas e Linguas Indígenas do Brasil," in *Educação e Ciencias Sociais* (Rio de Janeiro, 1957), pp. 1–102. It is translated and reprinted in Janice H. Hopper (ed.), *Indians of Brazil in the Twentieth Century* (Washington, D.C., 1967), pp. 79–165.

9 Ribeiro (1957), in Hopper, p. 86.

10 Ribeiro (1957), p. 86.

11 Ribeiro (1957), p. 86.

12 Ribeiro (1957), p. 87.

13 Ribeiro (1957), pp. 112–15.

14 Several sources, besides Ribeiro (1962, 1970), discuss the general demoralization that took place in the SPI in the late 1950s. See: Carlos de Araújo Moreira Neto, "Relatorio Sobre a Situação Atual dos Indios Kayapós," *Revista de Antropologia*, 11, Nos. 1 and 2 (São Paulo, 1959), 49–64; Alfred Metraux, "Disaparition des Indiens dans le Bresil Central," *Bulletin of the International Committee on Urgent Anthropological and Ethnological Research*, 5 (1962), 126–31; and Expedito Arnaud, "O Serviço de Proteção aos Indios: Normas e Implicações," *Museu Paraense Emilio Goeldi, Publicações Avulsas*, No. 20 (Belém, 1973), 71–88.

15 Francis B. Kent, "Brazilians Indignant at Indian Genocide Report," *Los Angeles Times* (March 22, 1968).

16 Paul L. Montgomery, "Killing of Indians Charged in Brazil," *New York*

Times (March 21, 1968).

17 The report by Braun is cited in the article: "Germ Warfare Against Indians is Charged in Brazil," *Medical Tribune and Medical News* (December 8, 1969).

18 Norman Lewis, "Genocide – From Fire and Sword to Arsenic and Bullets, Civilization Has Sent Six Million Indians to Extinction," *Sunday Times* (London), (February 23, 1969).

19 The *Jornal do Brasil* quotation was cited in Dom Bonafede, "Guards Turned Slaughterers of Brazil's Indians," *Washington Post* (June 9, 1968). For some examples of French reactions to the Figueiredo Report, see: "Le service brésilien de protection des Indiens s'est livré a un véritable génocide," *Le Monde* (March 15, 1968); "Open Letter to His Excellency General Arthur Costa e Silva, President of Brazil," *Current Anthropology*, 9, No. 5 (December 1968), 542; and Lucien Bodard, *Le Massacre des Indiens* (Paris, 1969).

20 Marcio Moreira Alves, *A Grain of Mustard Seed: The Awakening of the Brazilian Revolution* (Garden City, N.Y., 1973), p. 181.

21 Francis B. Kent, "Brazil Gets Inquiries on Alleged Indian Slayings," *Los Angeles Times* (March 29, 1968).

22 Quoted in William H. Ellett, "Pioneering the Amazon," *Americas* (October 1972), 24.

23 "For Brazil, Huge Projects to Fit a Big Country," *New York Times* (January 25, 1971).

24 Robert Moss, "The Moving Frontier: A Survey of Brazil," *The Economist* (September 1972), 1–78.

25 "Brazil: Striving to Become an Export Superpower," *Business Week* (January 12, 1974), 32.

26 Business International Corporation, *Brazil, New Business Power in Latin America* (1971), p. 1.

27 See, for example, the box titled, "Brazil's Vanishing Indians," that appeared in the article "Conquest of the Amazon: How High a Price?" *Newsweek* (July 3, 1972), 12.

28 International Committee of the Red Cross, *Report of the ICRC Medical Mission to the Brazilian Amazon Region* (Geneva, 1970); Primitive People's Fund/Survival International, *Report of a Visit to the Indians of Brazil* (London, 1971); and Aborigines Protection Society of London, *Tribes of the Amazon Basin in Brazil, 1972* (London, 1973).

29 Ribeiro (1957), p. 100.

30 Ribeiro (1962), p. 101.

31 Ribeiro (1957), p. 100.

2. Development plans in the postwar period

1 John W. F. Dulles, *Vargas of Brazil: A Political Biography* (Austin, Tex., 1967), p. 208.

2 "President Vargas on the Amazon Region," *Brazilian American* (Rio de Janeiro, October 19, 1940).

3 "The Amazon River and the Task of Man – Conference of Amazon Countries," *Brazilian American* (Rio de Janeiro, October 19, 1940).

4 Frank D. McCann, Jr., *The Brazilian–American Alliance, 1937 to 1945* (Princeton, N.J., 1973).

5 U.S. Government Printing Office, *History of the Office of the Co-Ordinator of Inter-American Affairs* (Washington, 1947).

6 U.S. Senate, Committee on Foreign Relations, *United States Policies and Programs in Brazil*, Hearings Before the Subcommittee on Western Hemisphere Affairs (Washington, May 1971), p. 181.

7 Earl Parker Hanson, *The Amazon: A New Frontier?*, Foreign Policy Association, Headline Series, No. 45 (March 1944). For a discussion of the role of organizations such as the Foreign Policy Association in the formulation of U.S. foreign policy following the war, see: G. William Domhoff, "Who Made American Foreign Policy, 1945–1963?," in David Horowitz (ed.), *Corporations and The Cold War* (New York, 1969), pp. 25–69.

8 Hanson, pp. 42–3.

9 Hanson, p. 47.

10 Hanson, pp. 52–3.

11 Hanson, p. 81.

12 Hanson, pp. 72–3.

13 Hanson, p. 86.

14 Hanson, p. 86.

15 For other accounts, similar to those of Hanson, see: Carleton Beals, "Future of the Amazon," *Survey Graphic* (March 1941), 149–52; R. H. Sharp, "Amazon Basin, Rich New Frontier?," *Science Digest* (January 1946), 52–6; and P. van Dresser, "Future of the Amazon," *Scientific American* (1948), 11–15.

16 U.S. Department of State, *Cooperative Programs in Health and Sanitation*, Inter-American Series, Publication 3239 (July 1948).

17 Charles Wagley, *Amazon Town: A Study of Man in the Tropics*, 2nd ed. (New York, 1964), pp. 304–5.

18 Benjamin H. Hunnicutt, *Brazil Looks Forward* (Rio de Janeiro, 1945), pp. 360–1.

19 U.S. Department of State, *Cooperation with the American Republics in Civil Aviation*, Program of the Inter-Departmental Committee on Scientific

and Cultural Cooperation (Washington, D.C., 1947), pp. 33–41.

20 For a description of how this new air and road network affected Indians, see: "Aboriginal Obstacles," *Time* (January 29, 1945), 46; and "Indians Shoot at Plane," *Life* (March 19, 1945), 70–2.

21 Willard Price, "Amazonia – Granary Out of the Jungle," *New York Times* (July 31, 1949).

22 Otavio Guilherme Velho, *Frentes de Expansão e Estrutura Agraria* (Rio de Janeiro, 1972).

23 Wagley, pp. 308–9.

24 Wagley, p. 307.

25 John D. Wirth, *The Politics of Brazilian Development, 1930–1954* (Stanford, Calif., 1970); and Peter Seaborn Smith, "Petrobrás: The Politicizing of a State Company, 1953–1964," *Business History Review* (1972), 182–201.

3. The significance of the military coup of 1964

1 For a discussion of the Brazilian model of development, see: Celso Furtado, *Analise do Modelo Brasileiro* (Rio de Janeiro, 1972).

2 Background information on Brazilian mineral legislation is contained in "Itabira Iron and the Export of Brazil's Iron Ore," *Revista Brasileira de Economia*, 24, No. 4 (1970), 157–74.

3 Edie Black and Fred Goff, "The Hanna Industrial Complex: Operations in Brazil," in *NACLA's Latin American and Empire Report* (New York, 1969), pp. 1–6. Also: "Iron Ore Deal Raises Squabble," *Business Week* (July 23, 1960), 90–2.

4 "Immovable Mountains," *Fortune* (April 1965), 55–6.

5 Black and Goff, p. 4.

6 Raymond Mikesell, "Iron Ore in Brazil: The Experience of Hanna Mining Company," in Raymond Mikesell (ed.), *Foreign Investment in the Petroleum and Mineral Industries* (Baltimore, 1971), pp. 345–64. Also: "Rip Van Hanna, How a Sleepy Cleveland Relic Became a Wide-Awake Global Entrepreneur," *Forbes* (April 15, 1973), 7.

7 "Brazilian Iron Miners Riding High," *Metals Week* (April 26, 1971), 10.

8 For background information on early foreign interest in the mineral resources of the Amazon Basin, see: Max Winkler, *Investments of United States Capital in Latin America* (Boston, 1928). Also: Arthur Cesar Fereira Reis, *A Amazônia e a Cobiça International* (São Paulo, 1960).

9 Yvonne Thayer, "The Carajas Iron Ore Project – A Boost to Amazon Development," *Brazilian Business* (August 1972), 13–14. Also: "Behind the Scene at Carajas: The Geological Picture and Details of the Iron Ore Discovery," *Engineering and Mining Journal* (November 1975), 151–2.

10 Marsha Miliman, "Brazil: Let Them Eat Minerals," in NACLA's *Latin America and Empire Report* (New York, 1973), pp. 3–13. Also: Ernest McCrary, "The Amazon Basin – New Mineral Province for the 70s," *Engineering and Mining Journal* (February 1972), 80–3.

11 Juan de Onis, "Brazil is Rolling Back the Amazon Jungle," *New York Times* (January 17, 1966).

12 The SUDAM legislation is contained in Law No. 5, 174, "Fiscal Incentives for the Development of the Amazon Region," dated October 27, 1966.

13 See Charles J. V. Murphy, "King Ranch South of the Border," *Fortune* (July 1969), 132–6.

14 Juan de Onis, "Brazil Begins Project to Develop Amazon Basin," *New York Times* (December 4, 1966).

15 James Nelson Goodsell, "Brazil Leaders Plan to Tame and Develop Vast Amazonia," *Christian Science Monitor* (January 10, 1967).

16 "A Highway to Save the Stricken Northeast," *Business Week* (November 14, 1970), 34–5.

17 Affonso Henriques, "Amazon Giant," *Americas* (February 1972), 2–11.

18 Robert G. Hummerstone, "Cutting a Road Through Brazil's 'Green Hell,' " *New York Times* (March 5, 1972).

19 "Brazil: Imperial Road," *Latin America* (October 6, 1972), 319.

20 For an official government statement on the Trans-Amazon Highway, see: "Highway Across Amazon to Spur Integration and Development," Brazilian Government Trade Bureau (New York, 1970), mimeo.

21 João Paulo dos Reis Velloso, "Brazil Charts Growth Plan," *New York Times* (January 28, 1973).

22 For a general discussion of foreign aid and loans to Brazil, see Israel Yost, "Foreign Aid to Brazil: Priming the Pump and Waiting for the Trickle Down," in NACLA's *Latin American and Empire Report* (New York, 1973), pp. 14–22.

23 Figures cited in: Peter B. Evans, "The Military, the Multinationals, and the 'Miracle': The Political Economy of the 'Brazilian Model' of Development," *Studies in Comparative International Development*, 9, No. 3 (1974), 29.

24 Mauricio Vinhas de Queiroz, "Os Grupos Multibillionarios," *Revista do Instituto das Ciencias Sociais* (Rio de Janeiro, 1965), pp. 47–78.

25 Eduardo Galeano, "Denationalization and Brazilian Industry," *Monthly Review* (December 1969), 11–30.

26 Richard S. Newfarmer and Willard F. Mueller, *Multinational Corporations in Brazil and Mexico: Structural Sources of Economic and Noneconomic Power*, Report to the Subcommittee on Multinational Corporations, Committee on Foreign Relations, U.S. Senate (August 1975), p. 177.

4. The Villas Boas brothers and Indian policy in Brazil

1 The idea of distinguishing between various models of Brazilian Indian policy comes from Roberto Cardoso de Oliveira, A *Sociologia do Brasil Indígena* (Rio de Janeiro, 1972).

2 "Memorias de Orlando e Claudio Villas Boas," published in the Brazilian magazine *Visão* (February 10, 1975), 24–39.

3 Orlando and Claudio Villas Boas, *Xingu: The Indians, Their Myths* (New York, 1973), p. 13.

4 Villas Boas (1973), p. 14.

5 Orlando and Claudio Villas Boas, "Saving Brazil's Stone Age Tribes from Extinction," *National Geographic Magazine*, 134, No. 3 (September 1968), 424–44.

6 Pedro Agostinho da Silva, "Information Concerning the Territorial and Demographic Situation in the Alto Xingu," in W. Dostal (ed.), *The Situation of the Indian in South America* (Geneva, 1972), pp. 252–4.

7 Roberto Cardoso de Oliveira, "Relatorio de Uma Investigacão Sobre Terras em Mato Grosso," in *SPI 1954* (Rio de Janeiro, 1955), pp. 173–84.

8 Agostinho da Silva, pp. 267–9.

9 Noel Nutels, "Medical Problems of Newly Contacted Indian Groups," in Pan American Health Organization, *Biomedical Challenges Presented by the American Indian* (Washington, D.C., 1968), pp. 68–76.

10 Orlando and Claudio Villas Boas (1973), p. 3.

11 Eduardo Galvão and Mario F. Simões, "Mudança e Sobrevivência no Alto Xingu Brasil-Central," *Revista de Antropologia*, No. 14 (São Paulo, 1966), 37–52.

12 Carmen Junqueira, *The Brazilian Indigenous Problem and Policy: The Example of the Xingu National Park*, International Work Group for Indigenous Affairs (Copenhagen/Geneva, 1973), p. 25.

13 A discussion of the reserve policy of FUNAI is contained in Aborigines Protection Society of London, *Tribes of the Amazon Basin in Brazil: 1972* (London, 1973), pp. 124–6.

14 Law No. 5.371, Brazilian National Indian Foundation (December 5, 1967).

15 Quoted in the Brazilian magazine *Visão* (April 26, 1971), 26.

16 Roberto Cardoso de Oliveira (1972), pp. 61–76.

17 Aborigines Protection Society, pp. 133–5.

18 For an official statement of Indian policy along the Trans-Amazon Highway, see: Brazilian National Indian Foundation (FUNAI), *Supysáua: O Indio Brasiliero* (Rio de Janeiro, 1970).

19 Brazilian Indian Statute, Article 20, Section 1, (a) through (f), English

translation, dated December 19, 1973. See also: Joseph Novitski, "Brazil is Seen Moving Toward Forced Relocation of Tribes," *New York Times* (July 14, 1971).

20 Quoted in the Brazilian newspaper *O Globo* (March 6, 1971). See also: the statement signed by eighty Brazilian ethnologists, anthropologists, historians, and sociologists on July 14, 1971, and reprinted as, "The Indians and the Occupation of the Amazon," in W. Dostal (ed.), *The Situation of the Indian in South America* (Geneva, 1972), pp. 338–42.

21 Official FUNAI notice of March 1971 on issue of Xingu National Park.

22 Quoted in the Brazilian newspaper *Folha da Tarde* (March 10, 1971).

23 Quoted in the Brazilian newspaper *Jornal do Brasil* (November 15, 1973).

24 Described in the Brazilian newspaper *O Estado de São Paulo* (December 16, 1973). See also: W. Jesco von Puttkamer, "Brazil's Txukahamêi: Goodbye to the Stone Age," *National Geographic Magazine*, 147, No. 2 (February 1975), 270–82.

5. Pacification expeditions along the Trans-Amazon highway network

1 Brazilian Ministry of Transportation, *A Construção do Brasil Gigante*, Special Report submitted to the Congress of the International Highway Federation (Brasília, 1972), p. 25.

2 Brazilian Ministry of Transportation, p. 65. See also: Joseph Novitski, "In Amazonia, The Army Are The Good Guys," *New York Times* (July 11, 1970).

3 Sarita Kendall, "The Development of Transport in Brazil," *Bolsa Review*, 6, No. 70 (October 1972), 540–50. See also: Nathan A. Haverstock, "U.S. Agency Loans to Brazil Worth $1 Billion," *Miami Herald* (January 28, 1973).

4 William H. Jones, "Brazil Mapping Amazon Jungle by Radar Sensing," *Houston Chronicle* (January 1, 1971). See also: "New Clues to the Resources in the Earth," *Business Week* (January 27, 1975), 116–20.

5 "Litton Maps Amazon," *Oil Daily* (October 10, 1972).

6 "Cats Slice Out a Highway in the Jungle," *Business Week* (January 8, 1972), 34.

7 Roque de Barros Laraia and Roberto da Matta, *Indios e Castanheiros: A Empresa Extrativa e Os Indios no Medio Tocantins* (São Paulo, 1967), p. 35.

8 For a description of the initial FUNAI expedition to the Parakanân, see: "Transamazónica: Indios no Caminho," in the Brazilian magazine *Veja* (December 8, 1970).

9 Aborigines Protection Society of London, *Tribes of·the Amazon Basin in Brazil: 1972* (London, 1973), p. 89.

10 "The Politics of Genocide Against the Indians of Brazil," document presented at the XLI International Congress of Americanists, Mexico City (1974). Reprinted in: INDIGENA and American Friends of Brazil, *Supysáua: A Documentary Report on the Conditions of Indian Peoples in Brazil* (Berkeley, Calif., 1974), p. 36.

11 "Brazil Indian Specialist Assails Policies, Resigns," *Miami Herald* (May 24, 1972).

12 The interview with Antonio Cotrim following his resignation from FUNAI appeared in *Veja* (May 31, 1972), 20–1.

13 Quoted in *Veja* interview, p. 21.

14 Aborigines Protection Society, p. 90.

15 Aborigines Protection Society, pp. 89–90.

16 For a description of early contacts with the Kréen-Akaróre, see: Adrian Cowell, *The Tribe That Hides From Man* (New York, 1974). Also, by the same author, *The Heart of the Forest* (New York, 1961).

17 Two special reports on the expedition of the Villas Boas brothers to the Kréen-Akaróre appeared in *Veja* (November 8, 1972), 44–60; and (February 14, 1973), 16–25.

18 For North American newspaper reports on the encounter with the Kréen-Akaróre, see: "Civilization Greets Lost Tribe of Amazons With a Giant Hug," *Boston Globe* (February 7, 1973); Marvine Howe, "An Amazon Tribe Takes a Step Out," *New York Times* (February 11, 1973); and "Party Meets Legendary Brazil Tribe," *Los Angeles Times* (February 25, 1973).

19 Quoted in *Jornal do Brasil* (February 6, 1973).

20 *Jornal do Brasil* (February 6, 1973).

21 "President Médici of Brazil Signs a Decree Creating a Temporary Reservation for the Giant Kréen-Akaróre Indians," *Los Angeles Times* (March 11, 1973).

22 The report by Ezequias Paulo Heringer on the conditions of the Kréen-Akaróre was quoted in the Brazilian newspaper *O Estado de São Paulo* (January 6, 1974).

23 Orlando and Claudio Villas Boas, "Saving Brazil's Stone Age Tribes From Extinction," *National Geographic Magazine*, 134, No. 3 (September 1968), 424–44.

24 W. Jesco von Puttkamer, "Brazil's Kréen-Akaróres: Requiem for a Tribe?," *National Geographic Magazine*, 147, No. 2 (February 1975), 254–68.

25 Edwin Brooks, "The Brazilian Road to Ethnicide," *Contemporary Review*, 224, No. 1300 (May 1974), 8. See also, by the same author: "Frontiers of

Ethnic Conflict in the Brazilian Amazon," *International Journal of Environmental Studies*, 7 (1974), 63–74.

26 This position was forcibly expressed in a document issued by eighty Brazilian ethnologists, anthropologists, historians, and sociologists on July 14, 1971. "To the extent to which the indigenous groups are guaranteed the inviolable possession of their traditional territories, and the eventual transformation of their way of life proceeds in a gradual and harmonious manner," this document read, "the Indians will cease to be the habitual and 'necessary' victims of progress and will become its beneficiaries and collaborators." See: "The Indians and the Occupation of the Amazon," in W. Dostal (ed.), *The Situation of the Indian in South America* (Geneva, 1972), p. 340.

6. The invasion of the Aripuanã Indian Park

1 Aborigines Protection Society of London, *Tribes of the Amazon Basin in Brazil: 1972* (London, 1973), p. 147.

2 Janice H. Hopper (ed.), *Indians of Brazil in the Twentieth Century*, pp. 18–19.

3 Norman Lewis, "Genocide – From Fire and Sword to Arsenic and Bullets, Civilization Has Sent Six Million Indians to Extinction," *Sunday Times* (London) (February 23, 1969).

4 Quoted in Lewis.

5 Quoted in Lewis.

6 Allen Young, "Brazil Becoming Self-Sufficient in Tin," *Christian Science Monitor* (October 7, 1967).

7 Leonard Greenwood, "South American Tin Industry Could Be a Sleeping Giant," *Los Angeles Times* (October 12, 1970).

8 "Brazil Builds First All-Weather, Cross-Continent Road," *Brazilian Bulletin* (January 1968), 3.

9 "Rondônia, Capital do Estanho," *Visão* (August 28, 1972), 94–9. See also: "Tin Road Sparks Boom," *Brazilian Bulletin* (August 1972), 8; and "Brazil: More Tin," *Mining Journal* (February 25, 1972), 160.

10 W. Jesco von Puttkamer, "Brazil Protects Her Cintas Largas," *National Geographic Magazine*, 140, No. 3 (September 1971), 420–44.

11 The decree establishing the Aripuanã Indian Park is numbered 62.995 and dated July 16, 1968. It mistakenly mentions the Nambikuára, rather than the Suruí tribe, as the other Indian group, along with the Cintas Largas, inhabiting the area of the park. Article 5 of this decree specifically mentions the status of mineral reserves found on Indian lands.

12 Quoted in *Jornal do Brasil* (December 3, 1971).

13 Leonard Greenwood, "Survivor of Brazil Indian Attack Tells of Slaying of

Two by Raiders," *Los Angeles Times* (March 15, 1972). See also, by the same author, "Fear Pervades Remote Brazil Indian Outpost," *Los Angeles Times*, (March 17, 1972).

14 Quoted in Leonard Greenwood, "Brazil Indian Expert Ousted Over Protests," *Los Angeles Times* (March 16, 1972).

15 Aborigines Protection Society, pp. 46–7.

16 Chiappino's message was reprinted in the *Jornal do Brasil* (November 21, 1972). The Brazilian newspaper *A Folha de São Paulo* noted that mineral companies were prospecting in this area as early as April 28, 1970.

17 A more recent report notes that the Patiño Mining Company has increased its share in Cia. Estanífera do Brasil (CESBRA) from 30 to 100 percent and cites complaints that "it is exploiting cassiterite deposits in Rondônia in a predatory and wasteful fashion." See: "Foreign Appetite for Brazilian Minerals," *Latin American Economic Report* (March 28, 1975), 52.

18 Jean Chiappino, *The Brazilian Indigenous Problem and Policy: The Aripuanã Park*, International Work Group for Indigenous Affairs (Copenhagen/Geneva, 1975), pp. 13–18.

19 Chiappino, p. 25. For a more recent report on the situation in the Aripuanã Indian Park, see: Jonathan Kandell, "Brazilian Squatters' Inroads in Amazon Provoke Indians," *New York Times* (October 8, 1976).

20 Ernest McCrary, "The Amazon Basin – New Mineral Province for the '70s," *Engineering and Mining Journal* (February 1972), 80.

7. Indian policy and the Amazon mining frontier

1 Max G. White, "Probing the Unknown Amazon Basin – A Roundup of 21 Mineral Exploration Programs in Brazil," *Engineering and Mining Journal* (May 1973), 72–6.

2 "Project Radam Maps the Unknown in Brazil," *Engineering and Mining Journal* (November 1975), 165–8.

3 "CVRD: Charging into the Future With a Bundle of New Projects," *Engineering and Mining Journal* (November 1975), 110–15.

4 "Trombetas: Major Bauxite Reserves in Search of a Future," *Engineering and Mining Journal* (November 1975), 153–7.

5 "CPRM: A Catalyst in Brazilian Exploration Programs," *Engineering and Mining Journal* (November 1975), 169–71.

6 Leonard Greenwood, "Brazil Begins Work on 3,000 Mile Highway," *Los Angeles Times* (October 28, 1973).

7 A report on the FUNAI program in the northwestern part of the Amazon Basin appeared in the Brazilian weekly *Opinião* (March 5, 1973).

8 Aborigines Protection Society of London, *Tribes of the Amazon Basin in Brazil: 1972* (London, 1973), pp. 70–3.
9 Marvine Howe, "Indians Kill 3 in Raid on Brazilian Amazon Post," *New York Times* (February 2, 1973).
10 Marvine Howe, "Amazon Indians Kill 3 in Attack," *New York Times* (January 6, 1975).
11 Quoted in "Brazil Suffers Setback in Amazon," *San Francisco Chronicle* (January 7, 1975), from a *New York Times* release.
12 Quoted in "Death at Abunari Two," *Time* (January 20, 1975), 43.
13 Quoted in Leonard Greenwood, "Brazil's Chief Indian Scout Suspended," *Los Angeles Times* (January 8, 1975).
14 Quoted in *San Francisco Chronicle* (January 7, 1975).
15 Amancio's strategy for pacifying the Waimirí-Atroarí was described in Leonard Greenwood's article, "Brazil's Chief Indian Scout Suspended," *Los Angeles Times* (January 8, 1975).
16 Quoted in *Los Angeles Times* (January 8, 1975). See also: Marvine Howe, "Brazil Refuses to Punish Indians," *New York Times* (January 9, 1975).
17 "Brazil: A Road Into the Jungle," *San Francisco Chronicle* (February 1, 1975).
18 For a discussion of the situation of the Yanomamö on the Venezuelan side of the border, see: Jacques Lizot, *The Yanomami in the Face of Ethnocide*, International Work Group for Indigenous Affairs (Copenhagen, 1976).
19 Aborigines Protection Society, p. 63.
20 Aborigines Protection Society, pp. 65–6.
21 Edwin Brooks, "The Brazilian Road to Ethnicide," *Contemporary Review*, 224, No. 1300 (May 1974), 8.
22 "Uranium Discovery Threatens Yanomamö Tribe," *Brazilian Information Bulletin* (Berkeley, Calif., summer 1975), 6–10.
23 United Nations, *Stemming the River of Darkness: The International Campaign Against River Blindness* (New York, no date), p. 4.
24 R. J. A. Goodland and H. S. Irwin, *Amazon Jungle: Green Hell to Red Desert?* (Amsterdam, 1975), p. 55.
25 Quoted in *O Estado de São Paulo* (February 8, 1975).
26 Quoted in *O Estado de São Paulo* (March 1, 1975).
27 Quoted in *Jornal do Brasil* (March 5, 1975).
28 Paul Kemezis, "Bonn and Brazil in Uranium Deal," *New York Times* (May 3, 1975).
29 "South America: Anthropologists Go Home!," *Survival International Review*, 1, No. 15 (spring 1976), 26.
30 The recent cassiterite discoveries on Yanomamö lands were described in a

special report by Atenéia Feijó and José Moure in the Brazilian magazine *Manchete* (July 24, 1976), 66–77.

31 Brazilian Indian Statute, Title III, Chapter 1, Article 18, English translation, dated December 19, 1973.

32 For a discussion of the effects of U.S. Bureau of Indian Affairs land and resource policies on Indian tribes in the United States, see: Edgar S. Cahn and David W. Hearne (eds.), *Our Brother's Keeper: The Indian in White America* (New York, 1969), pp. 68–111.

8. The rise of agribusiness in Brazil

1 "Brazil: The Small Farmer Must Go," *Latin America* (May 17, 1974), 151.

2 William R. Long, "Brazil Pushing Development of Amazon Despite Warnings," *Miami Herald* (January 6, 1975).

3 "Brazil Pushing Jungle Land Rush," *San Francisco Chronicle* (January 12, 1975).

4 For an excellent description of the new ranches in central Brazil, see: Anthony Smith, *Mato Grosso: The Last Virgin Land* (New York, 1971). Also, the special issue of the Brazilian magazine *Realidade* on the Amazon, dated October 1971.

5 Pedro Casaldáliga, *Uma Igreja da Amazônia em Conflito com o Latifúndio e a Marginalização Social* (Mato Grosso, 1971), pp. 12–14.

6 Casaldáliga, p. 24.

7 Robin Hanbury-Tenison, *Report of a Visit to the Indians of Brazil* (London, 1971), p. 26. See also the more detailed discussion of conditions on the Ilha do Bananal in Hanbury-Tenison, A *Question of Survival for the Indians of Brazil* (New York, 1973), pp. 101–12.

8 Casaldáliga, p. 22. A discussion of the establishment of the Xavante community at São Marcos is contained in Aborigines Protection Society of London, *Tribes of the Amazon Basin in Brazil: 1972* (London, 1973), p. 29. See also: David Maybury-Lewis, *The Savage and the Innocent* (Boston, 1965).

9 Marvine Howe, "Brazilian Indians Get Guarantees," *New York Times* (September 24, 1972).

10 The attitudes of several Brazilian cattle ranchers toward Indians were cited in an article in the Brazilian newspaper *O Estado de São Paulo* (September 14, 1973). See also Hanbury-Tenison's description of a conversation with a North American cattle rancher who owned land occupied by members of the Xavante tribe, in Hanbury-Tenison (1973), p. 29.

11 Aborigines Protection Society, pp. 172–3.

12 Xavante chief Juruna quoted in the Brazilian newspaper *O Estado de São*

Paulo (July 22, 1973). See also: Marvine Howe, "Indian–Settler Conflict in Brazil is Said to Be Nearing Violence," *New York Times* (March 10, 1973).

13 "Brazil: Indian Drums," *Latin America* (November 16, 1973), 367.

14 Marvine Howe, "Brazil's Xavante Live Uneasily on Frontier's Fringe," *New York Times* (August 4, 1974). See, also, the interview with the Xavante chief Dzururan in *Veja* (November 20, 1974), 3–6.

15 Casaldáliga (1971), pp. 26–8. For other accounts of agricultural labor conditions in the Amazon, see: Jeff Radford, "Slave Labor in the Amazon," *San Francisco Chronicle* (October 22, 1972); and "Brazil Jungle Scene of 'Slave' Labor," *Christian Science Monitor* (January 27, 1975).

16 Casaldáliga, pp. 15–21.

17 Casaldáliga, pp. 60–3.

18 See the long memorandum dated September 2, 1970 by Father François Jentel, published in Casaldáliga, pp. 79–85.

19 Marvine Howe, "Amazon Priests Meet Resistance," *New York Times* (December 10, 1972).

20 Marvine Howe, "Church and State Clash in Amazon," *New York Times* (July 22, 1973). See also: Leonard Greenwood, "Sentencing of Priest Stirs Brazil Church," *Los Angeles Times* (July 17, 1973); and "Once-Imprisoned Priest Ordered Expelled by Brazil," *Miami Herald* (December 17, 1975).

21 Casaldáliga, p. 44. See also: "Assembly of Bishops Urges Defense of Human Rights in Brazil," *New York Times* (March 18, 1973).

22 The several World Bank loans to the agribusiness sector in Brazil are noted in *Latin America* (April 5, 1974), 107.

23 U.S. Department of Commerce, *Brazil: Survey of US Export Opportunities* (Washington, D.C., 1974), p. 60.

24 Herbert E. Meyer, "The Baffling Super-Inflation in Meat," *Fortune* (July 1973), 116–19.

25 "Amazonia is Developing in Every Direction," *Brazilian Bulletin* (August 1974), 4–5.

26 U.S. Department of Commerce, pp. 66–7.

27 "D. K. Ludwig Plans to Harvest a Jungle," *Business Week* (July 31, 1971), 34.

28 Jonathan Kandell, "The Expanding Empire of a Quiet Tycoon," *New York Times* (May 2, 1976).

29 Richard Armstrong, "Suddenly It's Mañana in Latin America," *Fortune* (August 1974), 138–43.

30 Marvine Howe, "VW Adding Cattle to Beetles in Brazil," *New York Times* (July 25, 1974).

31 For a more detailed discussion of Deltec's agribusiness investments in Brazil, see: "Deltec," *Brazilian Information Bulletin* (Berkeley, Calif., winter

1974), 17–19. Also, Deltec International Limited, *Annual Report*, 1972.
32 "Deltec is Selling Stake in 3 Brazilian Concerns to Group for $20 Million," *Wall Street Journal* (December 18, 1972).
33 Transnational Institute, *World Hunger: Causes and Remedies* (Amsterdam, October 1974).
34 "Brazil: The Dead Side of the Miracle," *Brazilian Information Bulletin* (Berkeley, Calif., winter 1974), 15.
35 Figures cited in *Jornal do Brasil* (July 7, 1973).
36 Quoted in *O Estado de São Paulo* (July 3, 1971).
37 Quoted in *Jornal do Brasil* (August 25, 1971).
38 "Brazil: Rich Man, Poor Man," *Latin America* (August 24, 1973), 268–9. The 1973 adult nutritional survey of São Paulo cited in the previous paragraph was referred to in this article.

9. The deforestation of the Brazilian Amazon

1 R. J. A. Goodland and H. S. Irwin, *Amazon Jungle: Green Hell to Red Desert?* (Amsterdam, 1975). This study originally appeared under the title, "An Ecological Discussion of the Environmental Impact of the Highway Construction Program in the Amazon Basin," *Landscape Planning*, 1, Nos. 2 and 3 (1974), 123–254.
2 Leonard Greenwood, "Brazil Warned of Amazon Destruction," *Los Angeles Times* (May 25, 1975). See also: "Brazilian Survey Results," *Latin America Economic Report* (June 6, 1975), 88, which noted that the Project Radam Survey revealed that only 4.02 percent of the surface of the jungle had medium- to high-fertility soils, and that 79.89 percent of the area was under water for at least part of the year.
3 Superintendency for the Development of the Amazon (SUDAM), *Estudos Básicos Para o Estabelecimento de Uma Política de Desenvolvimento dos Recursos Florestais e de Uso Racional das Terras na Amazônia* (Belém, 1974). This document was a basic position paper on the need to promote commercial forestry operations in the Amazon. See also: "Brazilian Pulp and Cellulose," *Latin America Economic Report* (June 14, 1974), 91.
4 Many of the ideas in this chapter came from an attempt to apply Barry Commoner's writings on the "environmental crisis" to the case of the Brazilian Amazon. See particularly: Barry Commoner, *The Closing Circle: Nature, Man, and Technology* (New York, 1971).
5 Felisberto C. de Camargo, "Report on the Amazon Region," in UNESCO, *Problems of Humid Tropical Regions* (Paris, 1958), pp. 11–24.
6 Betty J. Meggers, *Amazonia: Man and Culture in a Counterfeit Paradise* (Chicago, 1971), p. 158.

7 Harald Sioli, "Recent Human Activities in the Brazilian Amazon Region and Their Ecological Effects," in Betty J. Meggers, Edward S. Ayensu, and W. Donald Duckworth (eds.), *Tropical Forest Ecosystems in Africa and South America: A Comparative View* (Washington, D.C., 1973), p. 321.

8 Sioli (1973), pp. 323–4.

9 Meggers (1971), p. 14. Most of the discussion of *terra firme* ecology that follows comes from this source unless otherwise noted.

10 The classic work on this subject is P. W. Richards, *The Tropical Rainforest: An Ecological Study* (Cambridge, U.K., 1952). For more recent accounts, see: C. F. Jordan, "Productivity of the Tropical Rainforest and its Relation to a World Pattern of Energy Storage," *Journal of Ecology*, 59 (1971), 127–42; and N. Stark, "Nutrient Cycling II: Nutrient Distribution in Amazonian Vegetation," *Tropical Ecology*, 12 (1971), 177–201.

11 Data reported in Meggers (1971), p. 17.

12 Sioli (1973), pp. 321–34. See also the discussion of deforestation and agriculture in Goodland and Irwin (1975), pp. 23–47.

13 Felisberto C. de Camargo, "Terra e Colonização no Antigo e Novo Quaternario na Zona de Estrada de Ferro de Bragança, Estado do Pará-Brasil," *Boletim Museu Pará Emilio Goeldi*, 10 (1948), 123–47.

14 Eugenia Gonçalves Egler, "A Zona Bragantina no Estado do Pará," *Revista Brasileira da Geografia*, 23 (1961), 527–55.

15 Mary McNeil, "Lateritic Soils in Distinct Tropical Environments: Southern Sudan and Brazil," in M. Taghi Farvar and John P. Milton (eds.), *The Careless Technology: Ecology and International Development* (Garden City, N.Y., 1972), pp. 603–7.

16 Mary McNeil, "Lateritic Soils," *Scientific American* (November 1964), 96–102.

17 Figures cited in the special issue of *Realidade* (October 1971), 144.

18 For a discussion of recent trends in tractor production in Brazil, see: U.S. Department of Commerce, *Brazil: Survey of US Export Opportunities* (Washington, D.C., 1974), pp. 53–4.

19 Deborah Shapley, "Herbicides: Agent Orange Stockpile May Go to the South Americans," *Science*, 180, No. 4081 (April 6, 1973), 43–5. See also: Morton Mintz, "Scientists Bare Perilous Chemical in Vietnam Defoliant," *Washington Post* (April 6, 1973); and Adams Schmidt, "Unloading Leftover Defoliants," *Christian Science Monitor* (April 28, 1973).

20 Quoted in the *Jornal do Brasil* (May 19, 1974). The usage of chemical herbicides by cattle ranchers in the Amazon is also noted in Charles Venhecke, "Taming Brazil's Wild West," *Atlas* (July 1975), 15–19.

21 Quoted in "What Shall We Do to Save Amazonia?," *Latin American Documentation Center Reports* (Washington, D.C., January 1974). See also:

W. Denevan, "Development and the Imminent Demise of the Amazon Rainforest," *The Professional Geographer*, 25, No. 2 (1973), 130–5.

22 Quoted in the Brazilian weekly *Opinião* (October 8, 1973).

23 Cited in "The Amazon Rain Forest is Said to be Threatened," *New York Times* (October 20, 1974).

24 Quoted in "Amazonia: Green Hell or Cornucopia?," *Latin American Documentation Center Reports* (Washington, D.C., January 1974).

25 Figures cited in *O Estado de São Paulo* (November 11, 1975), 60.

26 Sioli's calculations were first reported in the Brazilian magazine *Realidade* (October 1971), 146–9, and received a great deal of attention in the international press. For further discussion of this issue, see: Reginald E. Newell, "The Amazon Forest and Atmospheric General Circulation," in W. H. Mathews (ed.), *Man's Impact on the Climate* (Cambridge, Mass., 1971), pp. 457–9.

27 Sioli repeated these warnings in Goodland and Irwin (1975), preface.

28 SUDAM (1974), p. 4.

29 SUDAM (1974), pp. 10–21. A program for the technological modernization of the lumber industry in the Amazon was suggested several years before the publication of this report in Eugene P. Horn, "The Lumber Industries of the Lower Amazon Valley," *Caribbean Forester*, 18 (1967), 56–67.

30 SUDAM (1974), pp. 21–9. The large Georgia-Pacific, Bruynzeel, and Toyomenka lumber operations in the Amazon are described in "The Amazon: Its Treasures Are Being Revealed," *Brazilian Trends: Economic Development in Brazil* (1972), pp. 27–8. Recently, a Taiwanese Company, the Formosa Chemical and Fiber Corporation, also announced plans for the establishment of a large lumber and plywood project in the State of Pará. See: "Taiwan Plant for Amazon," *Latin America Economic Report* (May 16, 1975), 73.

31 SUDAM (1974), pp. 34–44.

32 For a discussion of several of the problems surrounding forestry management in the tropics, see: Raymond F. Dasmann, *Planet in Peril: Man and the Biosphere Today* (New York, 1972), pp. 161–3.

33 The economic and environmental reasons for the failure of the Ford plantations in the Amazon and the more ecologically adapted experiments carried out by the Agronomy Institute of the North are discussed in Sioli (1973), pp. 321–34.

34 A. Gómez-Pompa, C. Vásquez-Yanes, and S. Guevara, "The Tropical Rain Forest: A Non-renewable Resource," *Science*, 177 (September 1, 1972), 762–5.

35 For a discussion of the problems posed by these technologies in temperate-

climate countries, see: N. Wood, *Clearcutting: Deforestation in America* (San Francisco, 1971).

36 Machado's speech was quoted in Leonard Greenwood, "Scientist Hits Amazon Basin Development," *Los Angeles Times* (April 5, 1973). For a similar view, see: F. R. Fosberg, "Temperate Zone Influence on Tropical Forest Land Use: A Plea for Sanity," in Meggers, Ayensu, and Duckworth (eds.), p. 346.

10. The Amazon Basin: implications
for United States foreign policy in Brazil

1 Darcy Ribeiro, "Indigenous Cultures and Languages of Brazil," in Janice H. Hopper (ed.), *Indians of Brazil in the Twentieth Century* (Washington, D.C., 1967), pp. 95–6.

2 For a discussion of the important role that multinational corporations have assumed on a worldwide basis, see: United Nations, Department of Economic and Social Affairs, *Multinational Corporations in World Development* (New York, 1973). Also, Richard J. Barnet and Ronald M. Müller, *Global Reach: The Power of the Multinational Corporations* (New York, 1975).

3 Recent events in the northwestern part of the Amazon Basin are discussed in Shelton H. Davis and Robert O. Mathews, *The Geological Imperative: Anthropology and Development in the Amazon Basin of South America* (Cambridge, Mass., 1976).

4 The significance of this new land-occupation pattern in the Amazon came to international attention in July 1976 when John Weaver Davies, a large landowner and former colonel in the U.S. Air Force, was critically wounded and two of his sons killed by peasants in the Paragominas region of Pará. See: "Brazil: The Law of the Jungle," *Latin America* (July 16, 1976), 218.

5 The military offensive against the Catholic church in the Amazon is described in "Brazil: Fear of God," *Latin America* (December 24, 1976), 394. See also: Jonathan Kandell, "Brazil's Bishops Condemn Military Regime," *New York Times* (November 20, 1976).

6 For an intimate description of conditions in the Brazilian Northeast, and an account of the peasant revolt that occurred in this region previous to the military coup of 1964, see: Josué de Castro, *Death in the Northeast* (New York, 1966).

7 Jonathan Kandell, "Brazil's 'Miracle' Ignores Poor," *New York Times* (February 11, 1976). See also, by the same reporter, "Brazil's 'Miracle' Makes a Staple Scarce," *New York Times* (December 14, 1976).

8 Robert J. A. Goodland, "Is This Big Parking Lot Where Brazil Used to Have the Amazon Region?," *New York Times* (September 15, 1975).

9 "Controversy on Brazil–US Deal," *Latin America Economic Report* (May 28, 1976), 83. It is noteworthy that Secretary of the Treasury Simon's visit to Brazil occurred just months after the United States and Brazil signed an historic agreement to consult each other on all important political and economic issues involving both countries and their relations with the rest of the world. See: Jonathan Kandell, "U.S. and Brazil Sign Accord on Ties," *New York Times* (February 22, 1976).

10 U.S. Senate, Committee on Foreign Relations, *United States Policies and Programs in Brazil*, Hearings Before the Subcommittee on Western Hemisphere Affairs (Washington, D.C., May 1971). Unfortunately, it was not until several years following these hearings that revelations began to appear about possible U.S. government intervention in the Brazilian military coup of 1964. See the important documents described in David Binder, "U.S. Assembles a Force in 1964 for Possible Use in Brazil Coup," *New York Times* (December 30, 1976).

11 U.S. Senate, Committee on Foreign Relations, *Multinational Corporations and United States Foreign Policy*, Hearings Before the Subcommittee on Multinational Corporations (Washington, D.C., March 1973). See also: Richard S. Newfarmer and Willard F. Mueller, *Multinational Corporations in Brazil and Mexico: Structural Sources of Economic and Noneconomic Power* (Washington, D.C., August 1975).

12 U.S. House of Representatives, Committee on Foreign Relations, *International Protection of Human Rights*, Hearings Before the Subcommittee on International Organizations and Movements (Washington, D.C. 1974). See also: David Binder, "U.S. Urged to Act on Human Rights, House Unit Calls for Focus on Violations Abroad," *New York Times* (March 28, 1974).

13 Juan de Onis, "U.S. and Latins: Violations of Rights vs. Aid From Congress," *New York Times* (October 4, 1976).

14 For a more detailed discussion of these issues, see: Richard Arens (ed.), *Genocide in Paraguay* (Philadelphia, 1976). See also the various country studies of indigenous rights violations in W. Dostal (ed.), *The Situation of the Indian in South America* (Geneva, 1972). These studies, along with the present book, provide overwhelming evidence for the need to create new international mechanisms for the effective protection of aboriginal peoples' rights.

Bibliography

Aborigines Protection Society of London. *Tribes of the Amazon Basin in Brazil, 1972*. London, 1973.

Alves, Marcio Moreira. *A Grain of Mustard Seed: The Awakening of the Brazilian Revolution*. Garden City, N.Y., 1973.

Amnesty International. *Report on Torture*. London, 1975.

Arens, Richard (ed.). *Genocide in Paraguay*. Philadelphia, 1976.

Arruda, Marcos, de Souza, Herbert, and Afonso, Carlos. *Multinationals and Brazil: The Impact of Multinational Corporations in Contemporary Brazil*. Toronto, 1975.

Barnet, Richard J. and Müller, Ronald M. *Global Reach: The Power of the Multinational Corporations*. New York, 1975.

Bodard, Lucien. *Green Hell: Massacre of the Brazilian Indians*. New York, 1971.

Brooks, Edwin. "Twilight of Brazilian Tribes," *Geographical Magazine*, 45, No. 4 (January 1973), 304–10.

"Prospects of Integration for the Indians of Brazil," *Patterns of Prejudice*, 17, No. 2 (March–April 1973), 23–8.

"The Brazilian Road to Ethnicide," *Contemporary Review*, 224 (May 1974), 2–8.

"Frontiers of Ethnic Conflict in the Brazilian Amazon," *International Journal of Environmental Studies*, 7 (1974), 63–74.

Casaldáliga, Pedro. *Uma Igreja da Amazônia em Conflito com o Latifúndio e a Marginalização Social*. Mato Grosso, 1971.

Castro, Josué de. *Death in the Northeast*. New York, 1966.

Chiappino, Jean. *The Brazilian Indigenous Problem and Policy: The Aripuanã Park*. Geneva/Copenhagen, 1975.

Cowell, Adrian. *The Tribe That Hides From Man*. New York, 1974.

Dasmann, Raymond F. *Planet in Peril: Man and the Biosphere Today*. New York, 1972.

190   *Bibliography*

Davis, Shelton H. and Mathews, Robert O. *The Geological Imperative: Anthropology and Development in the Amazon Basin of South America.* Cambridge, Mass., 1976.

Denevan, William. "Development and the Imminent Demise of the Amazon Rainforest," *The Professional Geographer,* 25 (1973), 130–5.

Dória, Carlos Alberto and Ricardo, Carlos Alberto. "Populations indigènes du Brésil: Perspectives de survie dans la région dite 'Amazonie légale,' " *Bulletin de la Société Suisse des Américanistes,* 36 (1972), 19–35.

Dostal, W. (ed.). *The Situation of the Indian in South America.* Geneva, 1972.

Evans, Peter B. "The Military, the Multinationals, and the 'Miracle': The Political Economy of the 'Brazilian Model' of Development," *Studies in Comparative International Development,* 9 (1974), 26–45.

Farvar, M. Taghi and Milton, John (eds.). *The Careless Technology: Ecology and International Development.* Garden City, N.Y., 1972.

Frank, Andre Gunder. *Capitalism and Underdevelopment in Latin America.* New York, 1967.

Fuerst, René. *Bibliography of the Indigenous Problem and Policy of the Brazilian Amazon Region (1957–1972).* Geneva/Copenhagen, 1972.

Furtado, Celso. *Analise do Modelo Brasileiro.* Rio de Janeiro, 1972.

Gómez-Pompa, A., Vásquez-Yanes, C., and Guevara, S. "The Tropical Rainforest: A Non-renewable Resource," *Science,* 177 (September 1, 1972), 762–5.

Goodland, R. J. A. and Irwin, H. S. *Amazon Jungle: Green Hell to Red Desert?* Amsterdam, 1975.

Hanbury-Tenison, Robin. *A Question of Survival for the Indians of Brazil.* New York, 1973.

Hopper, Janice H. (ed.). *Indians of Brazil in the Twentieth Century.* Washington, D.C., 1967.

INDIGENA and American Friends of Brazil. *Supysáua: A Documentary Report on the Conditions of Indian Peoples in Brazil.* Berkeley, Calif., 1974.

International Committee of the Red Cross. *Report of the ICRC Medical Mission to the Brazilian Amazon Region.* Geneva, 1970.

Junqueira, Carmen. *The Brazilian Indigenous Problem and Policy: The Example of the Xingu National Park.* Geneva/Copenhagen, 1973.

Laraia, Roque de Barros and da Matta, Roberto. *Indios e Castanheiros: A Empresa Extrativa e os Indios no Medio Tocantins.* São Paulo, 1967.

Lévi-Strauss, Claude. *Tristes Tropiques: An Anthropological Study of Primitive Societies in Brazil.* New York, 1963.

Lewis, Norman. "Genocide – From Fire and Sword to Arsenic and Bullet, Civilization Has Sent Six Million Indians to Extinction," *Sunday Times,* London, February 23, 1969.

Lizot, Jacques. *The Yanomami in the Face of Ethnocide.* Copenhagen, 1976.

Maybury-Lewis, David. *The Savage and the Innocent.* Boston, 1965.

Meggers, Betty J. *Amazonia: Man and Culture in a Counterfeit Paradise.* Chicago, 1971.

Meggers, Betty J., Ayensu, Edward S., and Duckworth, W. Donald (eds.). *Tropical Forest Ecosystems in Africa and South America: A Comparative View.* Washington, D.C., 1973.

Newfarmer, Richard S. and Mueller, Willard F. *Multinational Corporations in Brazil and Mexico: Structural Sources of Economic and Noneconomic Power.* Report to the Subcommittee on Multinational Corporations, Committee on Foreign Relations, U.S. Senate. Washington, D.C., 1975.

Oliveira, Roberto Cardoso de. *A Sociolgia do Brasil Indígena.* Rio de Janeiro, 1972.

Peret, João Américo. *População Indígena do Brasil.* Rio de Janeiro, 1975.

Primitive People's Fund/Survival International. *Report of a Visit to the Indians of Brazil.* London, 1971.

Ribeiro, Darcy. "Culturas e Linguas Indígenas do Brasil," *Educação e Ciencias Sociais* (Rio de Janeiro, 1957), 1–102.

A Política Indigenista Brasileira. Rio de Janeiro, 1962.

Os Indios e a Civilização: A Integração das Populações Indígenas no Brasil Moderno. Rio de Janeiro, 1970.

Richards, P. W. *The Tropical Rainforest: An Ecological Study.* Cambridge, England, 1952.

Rosenbaum, H. J. and Tyler, W. G. "Policy Making for the Brazilian Amazon," *Journal of Inter-American Studies,* 13 (1971), 416–33.

Smith, Anthony. *Mato Grosso: The Last Virgin Land.* New York, 1971.

United Nations, Department of Economic and Social Affairs. *Multinational Corporations in World Development.* New York, 1973.

U.S. House of Representatives, Committee on Foreign Relations. *International Protection of Human Rights.* Hearings Before the Subcommittee on International Organizations and Movements. Washington, D.C., 1974.

U.S. Senate, Committee on Foreign Relations. *United States Policies and Programs in Brazil.* Hearings Before the Subcommittee on Western Hemisphere Affairs. Washington, D.C., 1971.

U.S. Senate, Committee on Foreign Relations. *Multinational Corporations and United States Foreign Policy.* Hearings Before the Subcommittee on Multinational Corporations. Washington, D.C., 1973.

Velho, Otavio Guilherme. *Frentes de Expansão e Estrutura Agraria.* Rio de Janeiro, 1972.

Villas Boas, Orlando and Claudio. "Saving Brazil's Stone Age Tribes From Extinction," *National Geographic Magazine*, 134, No. 3, September 1968, 424–44.

Xingu: The Indians, Their Myths. New York, 1973.

von Puttkamer, W. Jesco. "Brazil Protects Her Cintas Largas Indians," *National Geographic Magazine*, 140, No. 3, September 1971, 420–44.

"Brazil's Txukahamêi: Goodbye to the Stone Age," *National Geographic Magazine*, 147, No. 2, February 1975, 270–82.

"Brazil's Kreen-Akárores: Requiem for a Tribe?," *National Geographic Magazine*, 147, No. 2, February 1975, 254–68.

Wagley, Charles. *Amazon Town: A Study of Man in the Tropics.* 2nd ed. New York, 1964.

(ed.). *Man in the Amazon.* Gainesville, Fla., 1974.

Index

194 Index

204   Index